ANGKOR AND THE KHMER EMPIRE

ANGKOR
and the Khmer Empire

JOHN AUDRIC

ROBERT HALE · LONDON

© *John Audric 1972*
First published in Great Britain 1972

ISBN 0 7091 2945 9

Robert Hale & Company
63 Old Brompton Road
London SW7

To
Marian, Hilary and Jacqueline

Contents

Illustrations

PICTURE CREDITS

Ministère d'Information, Phnom Penh: 1, 3, 4, 21, 23; Musées Nationaux: 2, 10, 14; the author: 5, 6, 7, 8, 9, 11, 12, 13, 15, 17, 18, 19, 20, 22; Paul Popper Ltd: 16.

MAPS AND PLANS

Glossary

Apsara	Temple dancer
Atavar	Incarnation
Banteai	Citadel
Baray	Reservoir
Bodhisattva	One who is in process of becoming a Buddha
Brahma Buddha Indra Siva Vishnu	} See Chapter 6 "Four Gods Look Down".
Cardoman	Fruit of various plants of ginger family
Coriander	Plant with aromatic and carminative seeds
Cham	Native of Champa
Champa	ancient kingdom of Indonesia extending over south-east coastal region of modern Vietnam from Towane in the north to Cape Varella in the south
Cumin	Plant cultivated for its aromatic seeds
Deva	God
Devaraja	God-king
Devata	Goddess
Dvarapala	Temple guardian
Fennel	An unbelliferous plant. The seeds have an aromatic flavour
Garuda	Sacred bird with predatory beak and claws and human body
Gopura	Pavilion or stone platform in front of temple
Hamsa	Sacred goose
Harihara	A god; half Vishnu, half Siva
Hinayana	Buddhism of the Lesser Vehicle.
Jaya	Victory

Kambu	Mythical hero, ancestor of the Kambujas or Khmers (modern Cambodians)
Kambuja	Kingdom of Khmers (Cambodia)
Kompong	Village
Lakshmi	Vishnu's consort, goddess of beauty, riches and happiness
Laterite	A red porous rock composed of silicate of ammonia and oxide of iron
Linga	Phallic symbol, one of the manifestations of Siva
Lokapala	Regent
Lokesvara	The compassionate Bodhisattva
Mahabharata	Ancient Hindu epic or collection of poems, 110,000 couplets telling of the dynastic wars of the Pandara and Kaurava of northern India. With constant additions over the years looked upon as a kind of history of India
Mahayana	Buddhism of the Greater Vehicle, or collective works of the Buddhist School founded by Nagarjuna
Meru	A fabulous, sacred mountain in the centre of the world, containing the ashes of the gods. The home of the gods
Myrobalin	A dried astringent, prune-like fruit
Naga	A deified snake; the cobra in stylised form with multiple heads
Nagaraja	King of the *nagas*
Nandin	Sacred bull. Siva's mount
Parvati	Siva's consort
Phnom	Mountain
Prasat	Sanctuary tower
Rama	Incarnation of Vishnu, hero of *Ramayana*
Sita	Rama's wife
Stele	Vertical slab or column for inscriptions
Stupa	Funerary temple, spire
Surgriva	King of the monkeys, dethroned by Valin, his brother
Tevoda	Goddess
Vat, wat	Temple

ONE

Discovery of the Lost Capital

The ancient name for Cambodia is 'Kambuja'. Today, the term Cambodia is used when speaking of the country although in official circles in Phnom Penh the capital, the designation 'Khmer Republic' is quite common. The republic was created after the downfall of Prince Norodom Sihanouk, Head of State, in March 1970.

The inhabitants are known as Khmers or Cambodians, but there is a growing preference for the former name. It has always been popular. The educated classes, when pressed for the exact terminology have on the whole agreed over the years that it is Cambodia for the country, Khmer for the people.

The Khmers founded their fabulous capital at Angkor in the ninth century, but centuries earlier, in capitals they later abandoned, they had perfected an ingenious system of irrigation which was to be largely responsible for the amazing prosperity of the country. The wonderful and efficient water machines, the vast reservoirs in which the heavy rains and floods from the swollen Mekong were stored not only gave them abundant crop yields, but were a model of irrigation for other states in the region. The Khmers cradled the most brilliant civilization in South-east Asia. Angkor shone with a splendour unsurpassed by that of Babylon.

To defend their mighty empire, their warriors brought back scores of thousands of prisoners from their wars and set them to work building temples to the gods of the Hindu trinity-Siva, Vishnu, Brahma, and later the Buddha. They forced them to dig dykes, canals and build fortifications. Their mighty armies included the Royal Regiment of War Elephants, which numbered 200,000 of these huge, highly trained beasts. Weapons of war included fire rockets, arrow-firing machines, catapults and swords. The cavalry was the pride of the empire. The navy possessed numerous ships and armoured canoes.

For 600 years the empire, Moha Nokor as it was called, was the scourge of the region. The Khmers were the greatest slave dealers since the Pharaohs. In the thirteenth century the great empire, "the empire of a million elephants", controlled from Angkor had reached the height of its power and glory, and then began to decline. Repeated onslaughts by the warlike Siamese weakened it, and, unable to defend its borders and dependencies it slowly but inexorably disintegrated.

In A.D. 1431 the Siamese launched an all-out attack. Their armies swept across the country, crushing all resistance, to reach the massive walls of Angkor. After a siege of seven months the capital was forced to capitulate. The following year the Siamese are said to have returned for more loot. They had taken away priceless treasures the previous year, and they believed that vast quantities still remained in the temples or were buried in the city. To their amazement, they found the capital abandoned. As the years passed, Angkor became known as the 'Lost Capital'. Historians of many nations have advanced conflicting theories to account for its disappearance, and even today its sudden collapse still mystifies students of Khmer history.

However, after 400 years the jungle yielded up its secrets. In January 1861, Henri Mouhot, a French naturalist was hacking a path through the dense Cambodian jungle when he came upon the ruins of huge temples and towers in stone. Long dark battlements appeared to stretch unending into the jungle. There were magnificent galleries and bas-reliefs. Five majestic towers of breathless loveliness and shaped like lotus buds soared high above the surrounding devastation. Stone lions had fallen from temple entrances. Giant faces had been crushed or split by the encircling branches. The lovely, smiling faces of temple dancers peered at him from crumbling walls and foliage.

There were over 200 massive monuments. Huge trees had burst through the stout ornate ceilings and roofs. Roots, over 30 feet long, and some as thick as a man's thigh, groped and probed, twisted and twined along the walls of buildings.

Henri Mouhot was overcome with excitement. He had found the 'Lost Capital'. He lost no time in putting his discovery into writing, but he was not, as is widely believed to be the case, the first to find the ruins of Angkor.

In the middle of the sixteenth century a Portuguese missionary described the "forest of huge and terrifying ruins of palaces, halls and temples, of a size which would be unbelievable if he had not seen them", but his story was received with incredulity. Later, in 1604, another Portuguese priest, Quiroga de San Antonio, reported on similar lines, but fared no better. Then in 1672, a French missionary, Père Chevreuil, described his discovery in some detail, named the place Onco. But the same attitude of scepticism persisted.

Henri Mouhot's descriptions were so graphic and detailed that the previous reports were remembered. Moreover, France by this time exerted enormous influence in Indo-China, and this rich and powerful country was not only interested in the discovery but was able to finance investigations into the claim. Expeditions were quickly dispatched. One, manned by Commandant Doudart de Lagrée, Francis Garnier and Jean Delaporte arrived in Angkor. Others, led by Jean Moura, Étienne Aymonier, Adhemare Leclerc soon followed. The story of the Khmers unfolded.

In his book, *Voyages dans l'Indo-Chine, Cambodge et Laos*, Mouhot tells us of the hardships he was forced to endure in his search in the jungle. He mentions his difficulties and frustrations.

On the first day, our carriages were overturned, and it seemed as if it would be impossible to proceed. This happened in the midst of frightful swamps, and the carriages sank up to the axle trees, the buffaloes up to their loins . . . we were constantly travelling through a swampy plain covered with a thick shady forest which reminded me of the enchanted forests of Tasso. One could almost imagine that from each tree some fairy might issue. I can easily conceive how the imagination of a pagan people might convert these retreats of huge and ferocious wild beasts into the abode of genii. Twenty times an hour the men who accompanied us, in addition to the drivers, were obliged to cut the branches or remove the trunks of trees . . . the Cambodians were in a state of astonishment at seeing us, and if I had not brought with me from Siam the two young men I should not have been able at any price to have induced a single person to accompany me. . . . Cambodia has a terrible character for its un-healthiness. . . . In passing through a village of which two-thirds of the inhabitants were Annamites, I was in danger of being taken prisoner by them and finishing my exploration in their dungeons. . . .

The previous year, the wagons belonging to the French mission-aries had been completely stripped, and the men who accompanied the caravans were bound hand and foot and sent to Cochin China.

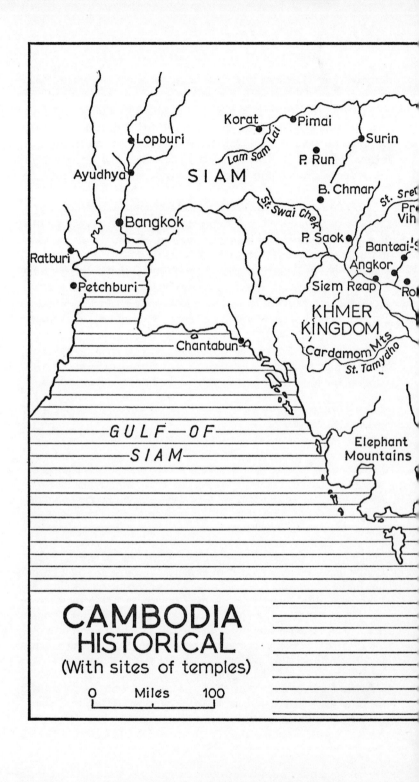

CAMBODIA
HISTORICAL
(With sites of temples)

0   Miles   100

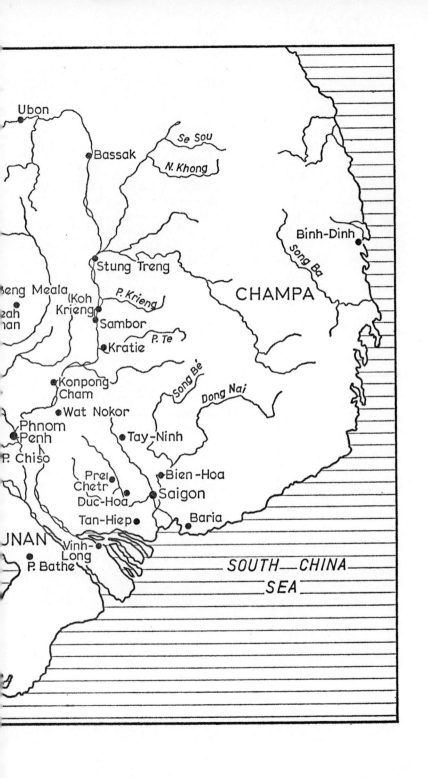

He finds the jungle most unpleasant. "During the rainy season, the men seldom go out on account of the leeches which multiply to such an extent in the woods as to render them inaccessible."

Even the assistance of the King of Cambodia does not smooth his journey to any appreciable extent:

Although the King of Cambodia had given us a letter in which he ordered all the chiefs of the Strokkhmer in Cambodia villages to furnish me with the means of transport on my route, I had much difficulty in arriving here because we could frequently find neither buffaloes nor carriages in the hamlets through which we had to pass, and because the Cambodians are the worst species of animal on the globe. Like the ass, they are not to be aroused from their lethargy, almost approaching stupidity, but by the application of the stick. Thus, I accomplished my journey which lasted nearly a whole month, that is three times longer than it would have taken me to go on foot.

However, his delight and excitement at his great discovery was surely more than adequate compensation for the hardship. He continues:

Nokhor or Ongkor was the capital of the ancient kingdom of Cambodia or Khmer, formerly so famous among the great states of Indo-China that almost the only tradition preserved in that country mentions that empire as having twenty kings who paid tribute to it, as having kept up an army of five or six million soldiers. . . . one of these temples, a rival to that of Solomon, and erected by some Michael Angelo, might take an honourable place among our most beautiful buildings. It is grander than anything left to us by Greece or Rome . . . unluckily the scourge of war, aided by time the great destroyer who respects nothing . . . the work of destruction and decay continues among those which still remain standing, imposing and majestic, amidst the masses of ruins all around. . . . the inscriptions with which some of the columns are covered are illegible, and if you interrogate the Cambodians as to the founders of Ongkor Wat, you invariably receive one of these four replies: "It is the work of Pra-Eun the king of the angels." "It is the work of giants." "It was built by the Leper King." "It made itself."

Henri Mouhot worked tirelessly amid the ruins, spurred on by the thrill of fresh discoveries. It must have been an eerie experience for him as he toiled in the silence, rewarded by glimpses of ornate gateways and majestic terraces which the tropical vegetation revealed only in parts, the remainder hidden under the centuries of uninterrupted growth.

He wrote: "... hardly a sound echoes but the roar of tigers, the shrill trumpeting of elephants and the belling of wild stags. ..."

However, it was a labour of love. He visualised architects, archaeologists and historians travelling from all over the world to Angkor to admire these shrines. He compared modern Cambodia, which he did not like, to the 'Lost Capital', as "being transported from barbarism to civilization, from profound darkness to light".

Auguste Pavie, in his book *Indochine 1879–1895*, wrote: "Your glorious past, my dear Cambodians ... can be compared with that of other illustrious countries, great and small. Chaldea, Assyria, Egypt, Greece and Rome. ... Nature is like a river. After bestowing upon you great posterity, you are now poor because her riches have been passed on. Other great empires, like Babylon suffered in the same way...."

Later, Paul Collard wrote: "A book in stone, a tangible document of history, they at least remain, the astonishing proof of a Cambodian civilization which has disappeared forever."

He was grateful for the enthusiastic support he received from the French teams and the interest shown by the French government. He compared his reception with that given to the vivid descriptions sent by the French missionary Charles Bouillevaux only twelve years earlier. He had written of their incredible size, majesty and beauty, but no one had been impressed. Mouhot now realised how depressed and frustrated these earlier explorers must have been. The 'Lost Capital' not only existed. They had seen it.

He was determined to keep alive the interest his discovery had aroused. He maintained that nothing had been done about this great heritage by the countries of South-east Asia. They were not interested. But the situation at that time was critical. Under constant threat from Vietnam on the one side and Siam on the other, Cambodia was in danger of annihilation. Mouhot pleaded that it was the duty of France to reveal to the world the wonders of this past civilization.

He expressed his fears eloquently: "... in one of the most remote countries of the world ... incomparable ruins, the only remaining signs, alas, of a lost race, forgotten, whose very name, like those of the illustrious men, architects and rulers who adorned it, appears destined to remain hidden among the chaos and ashes of the past".

Fortunately his fears were not realised. Angkor at that time was Siamese territory, but when the French first occupied Indo-China, a large part of western Cambodia including the province of Battambong was under Siamese control. The region east of the Mekong was ruled by the Vietnamese. Cambodia paid tribute to both powers. France allowed Siam to keep this western region and ceded Battambong and Siem Reap. The French colonial empire in Indo-China developed from her possessions of parts of Cochin China in 1862 to all of it by 1867. In July 1863, Admiral de la Grandière, as representative of Napoleon III, signed a treaty at Oudong by which the French protectorate was established over Cambodia. Later, her borders with Siam were adjusted and Angkor became French territory. Annam and Tonkin became part of the French empire in 1883 and the Laotian states in 1893. French domination was complete, but Siam was to preserve her independence to this day.

Mouhot did not live to see the march of history proceed at such a rapid pace in this part of the world. Nor did he see the miracle of reclamation, reconstitution and reconstruction accomplished by French archaeologists, architects, scholars and engineers. He died two or three years after his marvellous find. By one of those grim quirks of fate, the cause of his death was a tropical disease contracted during his search for the 'Lost Capital'. On his death-bed he told his friends, with grief and bitterness, that the secrets of the last days of Angkor had died when Angkor had died.

In his *Voyage d'Exploration en Indochine* Francis Garnier paints a bleak picture of the ruins. With Doudart de Lagrée he had visited them as early as 1866, 1867 and 1868. In the next few years which had followed on the news of Henri Mouhot's discovery, life had returned to Angkor. The great temple was inhabited, but by too many monks! *"Les prêtres sont trop nombreux pour suffire à l'entretien de l'immense temple. aussi doivent-ils se contenter de balayer chaque matin les galeries centrales les plus fréquentés et d'arracher une partie des herbes qui croissent entre les pierres. . . ."*

Sweeping out the most frequented galleries and weeding out between the stones!

The place stank. Almost entirely taken over by vegetation, birds and bats, who made their homes under the vaults and covered the floors with their droppings. *"L'odeur qu'ils répandant et la fiente dont ils recouvrent le sol de la galerie du premier étage rendent complètement inabordables certaines portiques de la partie nord."*

Most of the stone lions which decorated the stairways had been thrown down by successive invasions which brought about the decadence and downfall of the Khmer Empire. These were the monuments which were most easy to destroy. The rest were in little more than a mediocre state, either because they were mutilated where they stood or because they succeeded in weathering, without any shelter, all the rigours of the seasons.

Fortunately the central tower suffered the least, *"Quoiqu'il fût le plus élevé et le plus destructible. Le sanctuaire redouté qu'il contient a été sans doute un préservatif contre les envahisseurs et un stimulant à la piété réparatrice des habitants. . . ."*

The highest and the most destructible, and it survived because of the sanctity of its sanctuary which deterred the invaders and kept alive the piety of the inhabitants! It is doubtful whether the invaders would have been discouraged because of any reverence for the sanctuary, as subsequent explorers and archaeologists have since proved.

However, the tremendous work of reclamation was being organized. Angkor was to yield up her centuries-old secrets.

TWO

Birth of an Empire

When the Khmers were at the zenith of their power, their empire stretched from the South China Sea to the Gulf of Siam, including all modern Cambodia, eastern Thailand, Vietnam and Laos. Khmer monuments have been found all over this vast area. The recorded history of the ancient Khmers or Cambodians is mainly concerned with the lives of their kings, and the only sources of information are the numerous inscriptions they carved in stone. These told of their virtues and achievements. Sometimes a less illustrious individual was permitted a brief mention if the god-king graciously permitted. These inscriptions, the bas-reliefs, reports by Chinese envoys, and the splendid monuments left to posterity, tell the story of a master race and its fabulous capital.

Its history began before the commencement of the Christian era. Indian merchant adventurers sailed their ships to the shores of the countries which made up modern South-east Asia. These early voyages resulted in the emergence of states which at first were vassal dependencies of Greater India, although the Indians were not colonists but traders. The states adapted the Indian civilization to suit their environment and changing circumstances, and gradually evolved their own. The 'buried cities' of Ceylon, the multi-templed former Burmese capital at Pagan, the beautiful, majestic sanctuary of Borobadur in Java, and the greatest of them all Angkor Wat, the wonder of the world—all are monuments to this colourful, heroic and brilliant past.

India created several important cultures which lasted more than fifteen centuries. China and Islam were to unite in order to bring them down. René Grousset* wrote: "This conquest, these spiritual colonies represented by Borobadur and Angkor, constitute India's greatest title to fame, her contribution to mankind."

From the first century to the middle of the sixth, Cambodia

* *Histoire de l'Extrême-Orient*, by René Grousset.

was the centre of a Hinduized kingdom which ruled over a large part of the peninsula, and which the Chinese called Funan. This was a free translation of the Khmer word *phnom* which means 'mountain'. Throughout the centuries, the Cambodians spoke nostalgically of their original mountain homes.

The origin of Funan is more legendary than historical. The most popular story is that one night a heavenly spirit visited a handsome young Indian adventurer named Kaundinya in his sleep, and ordered him to sail eastwards with his bow and arrow. The next morning, Kaundinya remembered his dream and decided to visit the sacred temple where the wise counsellor lived. As he was about to cross the courtyard, he saw a bow and a quiver of arrows. He took this to be a sign that he should carry out the mission. Kaundinya then set off in a junk which was blown off its course. It was driven across the Bay of Bengal, through the Malaccan Straits, around the island known today as Singapore, up the South China Sea to the coast of Indo-China. The exhausted Indian thankfully sighted land, and as he was preparing to navigate his junk, he was astonished to see a canoe moving swiftly towards him. Seated in it was a most lovely girl. This was the native Queen Willowleaf, ruler of the country.

She was not smiling at him. Indeed, it was soon apparent that her intentions were hostile. Kaundinya, now thoroughly alarmed, realised that she was about to seize his craft, and with it his valuable cargo. He snatched up his magic bow and shot an arrow which passed right through the canoe. The young queen was both amazed and frightened. After a further and more prolonged demonstration of his magic, during which the canoe sank, her resistance crumbled.

Kaundinya, although lost in admiration at her beauty, was shocked to find that she went about completely naked although this was in accordance with the custom of her kingdom. He gave her a quantity of Indian silks and Indian jewels, which delighted her. It was not long before they were both completely in love. Their kingdom flourished.

There are several different versions of the legend. An old Khmer account claims that Willowleaf was a *nagini* or water spirit and belonged to the mythical *nagas* who were to become the guardian spirits of the Khmer Empire. Another, by the Chinese explorer K'ang T'ai who was sent to Funan in the third century, states that the kingdom was founded by Kaundinya whose name in Chinese characters was Hun t'ien. The capital was revealed to him in a dream which was to prove most accurate in so far as the chosen route was concerned. The kingdom was ruled by Queen Luiyeh (Willowleaf), who was a proud beauty. She had repelled all attempts by adventurers or others to land, by the simple expediency of sinking their boats and leaving the unlucky suitor to drown, or if he was more fortunate, to be picked up by one of her canoes and deposited on an uninhabited island. Kaundinya outmanœuvred her, sailed his ship into the harbour, sinking her canoe on the way. These tough measures paid off. They fell in love, were married and founded a dynasty which lasted for 150 years.

Yet another, an Indian version, tells of Kaundinya, a Brahman, who was given a javelin by Asvattharman, son of Drona. He threw it so that the place where it landed would be the site of his future capital. He married Soma, daughter of the *naga* king. Hence again, the adoption of the *naga* as the sacred symbol

Modern South-east Asia is populated by people of different nations with different languages and religions, although the latter is not bounded by frontiers. During the first century, the Buddhists and Hindus travelled from country to country preaching and proselytizing. The Christians followed. Nearly seven centuries later, missionaries from Islam arrived in the same region, where Indian and Chinese influences, culturally and politically were dominant. The Chinese settlers have kept up a steady stream since those early days. There are powerful minorities today making a valuable contribution to the economy of Laos, Cambodia, Burma, North and South Vietnam, India, Malaysia and Singapore. They hold fast to their ancient customs, and when they celebrate their festival days in these countries, business almost grinds to a stand-still.

The immigrants made their way into South-east Asia by several routes. Some took the sea voyage from the Coromandel coast to the Straits of Malacca, or followed the land route from India to China by way of Assam, Yunnan and Upper Burma. This land route was well established before the end of the first century. China set up a prefecture at Yung-Chang across the Upper Mekong. Ambassadors from the imperial court of Rome and Chinese, Buddhist and Hindu monks travelled in safety on the roads.

Only the most courageous sailed from the eastern ports of the Indo-Chinese mainland, for the sea route took them through the Malacca or the Sundra Straits, which was infested with pirates. The most savage punishments were inflicted upon those who were captured; imperial rescripts issued from Peking demanded an increase in the severity of the sentences, but they were not in any sense a deterrent. The pirates were excellent sailors, reckless and brave, and they set little value on human life. Moreover, the pickings were rich.

The land route, not unnaturally, was the one favoured by the majority. They travelled across the Kra Isthmus; they came from Tavoy over the Three Pagodas Pass, sailing up the Khanburi river to the valley of the Menam—an area, which was to be infamous because of the appalling suffering of allied prisoners of war at the hands of the Japanese when building the Burma railway during World War II. Another route, with similar dreadful memories was by way of Moulmein and the Rakeng pass. Large numbers found their way from the rivers Menam and Mekong, over the flat Korat plateau via Si Thep to the vast, fertile and densely populated Bassak district, the birthplace of the Khmer Empire.

By the end of the second century, well-defined states or kingdoms had taken shape in three regions: the lower Mekong and its delta, modern Annam north of Hué, and the northern part of the Malay peninsula.

The settlements of the kingdom of Funan had been built along the Mekong between Chaudoc and Phnom Penh. The Cambodians were to owe much to the Indians, for it was with their skill, industry and guidance that the foundations of Funan were so firmly laid.

They built an irrigation and drainage system which rapidly transformed much of the Mekong delta from barren swamps into rich, agricultural land. It was a work of great magnitude, ingenuity and organization, for some hundreds of canals had to be constructed, and the main sewers stretched for more than 100 miles. The sluggish waters were drained off into the sea, and rice fields flourished and yielded excellent crops.

The inhabitants lived in large lake cities, with rice and fish in abundance. These towns were fortified by huge earthworks divided by moats swarming with crocodiles. Houses were built on stilts or piles. Communication between the houses and different parts of the city was by a system of canals, which also linked the towns and provided access to the sea. These canals were of sufficient width and depth to take all ships, regardless of size. They sailed in from the sea, up the canals to berth right in the town itself. In this way, the town was both a port and a commercial centre. As more immigrants arrived, settlements developed in the kingdom proper and along the Mekong between Chaudoc and Phnom Penh. Towards the end of the second century there was a population explosion. Funan became a great economic and political power.

For some years its capital was Vyadhapura or 'the city of the hunters'. Oc Eo, its main port, was a sprawling mass of dwellings. It was an important harbour, busy and rich and used by ships trading with Malaya, Indonesia, Persia, India and the Gulf of Siam. It owed much of its prosperity to its strategic position on the sea route between China and the West.

Fan Shih-Man is believed to be the first King of Funan. He was determined to extend the kingdom, and he led his armies against neighbouring states. In most of his wars of aggression he was victorious. It was during his reign that the Khmers showed evidence of their skill in building, which throughout their history was to be an outstanding characteristic of their race. He brought back large numbers of prisoners from his wars, and set them to work building more fortifications and canals. Fan Shih-Man was killed while leading a campaign against Chen-lin, or the Frontier of Gold. The region of Indo China was known to the Indians as Suvarnabhumi, which is Sanskrit for 'Golden Land'. The reason for this is that large deposits of gold were found in the territory now formed by Cambodia, Burma, Thailand, Laos, Malaysia and Vietnam.

He was succeeded by Fan Chan. The term *Fan* corresponds to the Sanskrit suffix *Varman*, which was used by the dynasties of South-east Asia. He ruled for about twenty years. His policy was to consolidate the military gains of his predecessor and to establish good relations with mighty China. In A.D. 243 he sent an embassy with musicians and costly gifts to Peking, and was encouraged and delighted by the friendly reception it received. The embassy found life in the imperial city very pleasant, and extended its stay. Fan Chan did not live to welcome the imperial emissaries which Peking sent as an act of reciprocity and recognition a year later, and this duty fell to his successor, Fan Hsun.

Peking showed considerable interest in the proud and prosperous kingdom, selected men of learning and discernment to stay in the country and send back periodic reports on its activities. They spent several weeks sight-seeing, and their comments were illuminating. After describing some of the walled cities, they stressed the enormous difference between the habitations of the important officials who lived in palatial residences, and the poor, whose dwellings they thought were very primitive. In their view, the people were "ugly, black and fuzzy-haired". Away from the capital, the majority went about naked, The visitors met those who were in the same state in the poor quarters of the capital. Apparently the officials passed the hint around, because gradually more and more people of all classes began to be seen in clothes, although in most cases these consisted of a cloth worn around the waist. The embassy was astonished to learn that taxes were paid in pearls, silver and gold, while even the poor ate from utensils of silver. They concluded their first report with the verdict that the region was rich; the people aggressive but disciplined, and possessing unusual skill, ingenuity and endurance in the craft of building at which they excelled.

Fan Hsun was not the military genius his predecessor had been, but he was a master of intrigue. He was careful to maintain the good relations with China which had been a feature of the last reign, and at the same time he sought an alliance with Fan Hsiung, who had ascended the throne of Champa in A.D. 270. Throughout the next decade, they hurled their combined might against Tongking.

Champa, known to the Chinese as Lin-yi, was the kingdom of the Chams, and, although it formed part of Funan, the people were already finding the central control irksome. They were well aware that their land was rich in natural resources, and this may have prompted their leaders to adopt a more obstructive attitude towards Funan. However, the wily Fan Hsun succeeded in keeping them fully occupied with wars beyond their frontiers, and developed a competitive spirit among his generals to bring about greater efficiency. He deliberately created jealousy and suspicion among rival claimants to the throne, and their subsequent internecine quarrels strengthened his own position.

For the next three centuries Funan prospered. Wars of aggression led to the acquisition of more territory and the subjugation of states which were reduced to vassal kingdoms, The peasants' lot at this time was not harsh. There was an abundant supply of wood at hand for the construction of their homes. The fertile fields and the numerous canals gave them rice and crops, as well as fish in adequate supplies.

From the end of the fifth century, successive kings attempted to pursue a more peaceful policy. The empire was strong, and they realised that further extensions would involve problems of defence. Lines of communications were already fully extended. Resources in ships and man power were already under a severe strain. Then China was stirring again.

It was decided to suspend the harsh conscription laws which had been in force for over a century, and as a temporary measure to ease the forced labour projects by which peasants were uprooted from their homes and sent far away to labour long hours in building roads and fortifications.

As it was no longer necessary to maintain a large army, taxes were reduced. This more liberal attitude did not meet with approval from the young, tough and ambitious generals who had returned from successful wars with masses of slaves and treasure, and there were angry protests. Some left the country and took service in Chenla, which was situated to the north and was a vassal state of Funan, although its kings had more than once demonstrated their opposition to its edicts. However, during the first half century of the era of peace, Funan entered an age of enlightenment, and the arts and crafts were given full scope. The skilled craftsmen—and Funan boasted a large number of them— worked with bronze, ivory, coral, silver and gold. Sculpture took its inspiration from living objects. The results of much painstaking labour, with the laborious use of primitive tools, were often quite oustanding in craftsmanship, accuracy and finish.

More land was brought under cultivation, the granaries were full, the rivers and canals were kept well stocked with fish. Temples and religious shrines were now built in brick and stone. Stone columns recorded in print the virtues of their kings and the victories of the armies.

To the cosmopolitan court large numbers of Indian and Chinese monks, craftsmen, and princes with their retinues journeyed. With the exception of their monks—and these were few—the Chinese had only one interest, and this was trade. Nor was it resented by the natives who were soon lost in admiration at the efficiency and industry of the settlers. Goods were sold, bartered, assembled at trading posts and transported with ease and efficiency in ocean-bound ships which sailed in from the sea and up the canals.

Those Chinese settlers who remained in the country were content to work for very little. They intermarried, but they were never assimilated. They remained Chinese, and continued to observe their ancient customs which they were careful to hand down to their children. And so it has continued right through the centuries. Wherever they made their homes, they quickly became a powerful minority which exercised a strong influence on the nation's economy, and even directed it. Often, the humble immigrant from China was to rise to one of the highest positions in the land. Mandarins, court officials, or Chinese of importance made only brief visits. Perhaps these more illustrious visitors knew that their compatriots in Funan would follow the same pattern. In any case, they came only to assess the trade potential, to judge the political situation, to accept the tokens of homage which the rulers paid to mighty China, and to make reports on life and progress. They little knew that they were to render a great service to the Khmers and to posterity, for it is largely due to their observations and judgments that we are able to piece together the history of the Khmer Empire and the fantastic, magnificent capital of Angkor.

Funan assimilated a large number of Indians. These immigrants brought their crafts with them and they taught them to the Khmers, who were basically not a creative race. Military glory had ranked too high in the minds of their leaders during the first three centuries to allow of more than a passing interest in the trades which the Indians knew more about than they did. They were content to leave it to them. When they were able to make a start on beautifying their capital, they borrowed the Indian style in art and architecture. They welcomed monks who had come from India to expound the laws and blessings of Hinduism and Buddhism. In short, Indian influence was to dominate Funan, and for centuries afterwards to play a large part in shaping Khmer civilization. However, Funan was already showing signs of decline. From a military standpoint, she had overreached herself. Life in the large cities was undisciplined. Corruption was rife.

Officials purchased their appointments. The morals of the people were lax. In court circles, debauchery spread and became more vicious. The vast network of irrigation canals and water works was neglected.

This decline might well have been only temporary, but unfortunately it coincided with renewed agitation from another Indianized state which had settled around the middle of the Mekong, and whose rulers had cast envious eyes on Funan for many years. This was Chenla, the seat of the principality of the Kambuja. Here, Indian influence was less pronounced. The capital of Chenla had been built near a mountain called Ling-Kia-Po-Po on which a temple had been erected and consecrated to the god Po-to-li, or Bhadresvara. The kings of Chenla continually offered human sacrifices at night to this god.

Towards the middle of the sixth century, King Bhavavarman of Chenla began to prepare for an all-out attack on Funan. This ruthless, but fearless son of the royal house of Funan had married the female heir to the crown of Chenla, and on the death of her father he became king. He knew that the empire was weakening. His spies had given him an accurate picture of the country: the weakened defences, the dissolute officials and the opposition among the masses to military service. Then Bhavavarman was convinced that the Funan kings had perpetuated a strategic blunder in concentrating the population in large cities without adequate rearguard defences. He told his generals that hostile armies could advance unopposed over the country and starve them into submission.

In A.D. 549 his opportunity came. Fearful floods swept central Cambodia. Entire cities were submerged, with an appalling loss of life. Large numbers retreated before the advancing waters to the higher regions of Central Cambodia. Cochin China became once more a vast desert swamp.

These disasters decided King Bhavavarman. He advanced on Funan. After a short and easy campaign in which cities surrendered without resistance, and others from distant regions sent envoys acknowledging his authority, he conquered it. Chenla which included Bassak is regarded as the real home of the Khmers, although, of course, it had for centuries been part of Funan.

A well-known Khmer legend states that the royal family of the Khmers originated with the marriage of the hermit Kambu

Svayambhuva with the celestial nymph Mera by the god Siva. This legend is at variance with that which describes the marriage of Kaundinya and the *naga* princess, and was probably put out to explain the name 'Kambuja', which the Khmers adopted as that of their country.

A version which is still popular today tells that a sorcerer named Dak guided Kambuc, a prince of Ayra Deca and son-in-law of Siva, to the kingdom of the *Nagas*, which was an enormous, crystal cave below the surface of the earth. King Cobra, surrounded by a large number of multi-headed serpents, ordered Kambuc to explain the object of his visit.

Kambuc faced the king unafraid, and in a loud voice which reverberated throughout the throne hall, cried: "I am Prince Kambu Svayambhuva from the land of Arya Deca. Princess Mera, the beautiful foster daughter of Siva, the great god, was my wife. But Siva, in a rage, destroyed the crops, and my people died of hunger. Siva took back my wife Mera, and alone in a desolate country my grief overwhelmed me, and I left. I travelled to the east, across high mountains and vast deserts until I came to the great river which flows through your forest. I continued on my journey until I met the magician Dak who handed me a talisman in the form of rice. If it is your will that I settle here and make use of this talisman to raise up a nation of servants to the high gods, I will gladly do so. If not, then kill me, for I can go no further."

For some days the king of the *Nagas* reflected. His daughter, however, had fallen in love with the handsome stranger, and pleaded with her father to spare his life. Her entreaties were successful. Kambuc married her and founded a kingdom in the river valley. The people were called 'Kambujas' or the children of Kambu. In time, the name changed to Cambodge and then to Cambodia. Today, the *naga*, or sacred multi-headed snake can be seen on temple buildings, its long body forming a balustrade, and its several heads reared up and fanned out. The *naga* is also seen in a protective position over the Buddha. The image is represented as seated on its coiled body and the heads form a fan over it, protecting it from the elements.

Finally, Bhavavarman is alleged to have belonged to the lunar dynasty which had been founded by Soma and Kaundinya. The marriage between the young king and the lovely princess was to be the origin of other legends which persisted for centuries in connection with Khmer royal traditions, for successive Cambodian kings claimed descent from the solar or lunar lines.

Cambodians of all classes are well versed in their country's legends and very enthusiastic about them. Perhaps this is not so surprising. What country is without them? It is the degree of credulity which varies. The itinerant story-teller never failed to hold his audience with stories of the handsome Indian adventurer who, after a long and dangerous voyage captivated the lovely princess and married her. It was rare for the hero to be other than Indian. A Chinese did not have the same appeal. The princess was usually of Asiatic origin.

Chenla now became the centre of government, but Bhavavarman and his brother continued their wars of aggression. The former governed from Chenla, and was known as the protégé of Siva. The Khmers worshipped a trinity of Hindu gods. These were Siva, Vishnu and Brahma. Each in turn passed through eras of popularity and decline.

Siva was the god of destruction and therefore of creation, for death was accepted as the mother of life. His symbol was the *linga*, or phallus. Vishnu was worshipped as the preserver of the universe, a benevolent god. Brahma was the least prominent of the trinity.

Buddhism came later. It was this friendly, compassionate philosophy which was to destroy the cult of the god-king, turn the warlike Khmers away from war and make a major contribution to the downfall of the mighty empire. One wonders what were the thoughts of the powerful priestly cult of the trinity in the last hours of the dying empire. Did they regret the freedom and tolerance they had given those monks of the saffron robe, not only in proselytizing, but in erecting Buddhist shrines in the sanctuaries of the trinity? Perhaps they were less surprised at the tremendous swing to Buddhism and its repercussions than were these monks. Religious tolerance was one of the most commendable features of the Khmers.

Hinduism at this time centred around Siva and Vishnu, and the various kings were often referred to as a protégé of one or the other of the two.

Bhavavarman's brother, Chitrasena took command of the land and sea forces. He was a brilliant strategist, and in ten years had gained several outstanding victories. Three influential states of

Angkor Wat amid the surrounding jungle

The god Vishnu on Mount Mandara: part of a bas-relief of the
Churning of the Sea of Milk

north-west Cambodia were forced to surrender. These were Cak Rankapura, Bhimapura and Amoghapura. Unfortunately, he was impetuous and reckless. His campaigns carried him farther from the capital, and in the flush of his successes he overreached himself. His armies could no longer defend the old Funan empire which stretched from Champa in the east to the Bay of Bengal in the west, with a large part of the Malay peninsula as well. Each fresh acquisition of territory required an army of occupation to defend it, and his resources were unable to meet the heavy demands thrown on them.

The Malay states sent emissaries to Peking asking for a defensive alliance. The Mon state of Dvaravati on the Menam defied Chitrasena, and appealed to Peking for help.

The mandarins in Peking advised the emperor that it would be beneath the dignity of the celestial court to send troops, even a token force to settle any dispute among the barbarians. At the same time they considered that the young, ambitious and rising empire was worthy of close study. It was decided to send spies to make a report, and also an envoy of minor rank who would drop a polite hint to Bhavavarman that the imperial capital was not unaware of the progress of events in Chenla, and deplored any policy which would split Chenla instead of uniting it.

Bhavavarman received the envoy with much ceremony, and took care to show due humility at the veiled reference to the might of the Celestial Empire and the significance of any edicts issued from the Forbidden City. In any case, he was well satisfied. His territory had been increased, and he realised that it was important to consolidate his gains. He instructed his brother to make a great show of retreating, as this would demonstrate to Peking his peaceful policy, but he was to withdraw to strategic positions. In actual fact, Bhavavarman was disturbed by reports of revolts in some states, and he desired to bring about a measure of unity to the empire and make Chenla a more grandiose capital. The Chinese envoy departed satisfied. Peking had not lost face.

A few years afterwards, Bhavavarman died. He had been a despot, but a benevolent one. He hoped that Siva would be satisfied with his reign and the temples he had built and would welcome him into the new existence to which his spirit had sped.

Chitrasena succeeded him. He was convinced that he was responsible for his actions to none other than the god Indra. He was

3

an ambitious king who was determined to extend the empire. He sent costly gifts to Peking in an effort to win favour, for he was well aware that the mandarins would be a little suspicious over the accession to the throne by one who had devoted so much of his life to war.

He then embarked upon an even more aggressive policy than that of his brother. He was enough of a realist to know that Peking would be unlikely to force him to hand back any newly acquired territories, especially if the tribute he sent arrived in the capital ahead of any such disturbing news. This line of reasoning proved to be as successful as his military strategy. His armies were victorious over a wide field. The returning soldiers marched under triumphant roofed columns. Outstanding builders as they undoubtedly were, the Khmers were never able to master the intricacy of the arch. Chetrasina conquered the Mon valley after a masterly campaign, and commemorated his victory by building *lingas* or phallic monuments dedicated to the god Siva. These *lingas* have been found all over the old Funan Empire, particularly along the Mekong.

His reign ended in 611. He had achieved much in his eleven years' rule. His son Isanavarman succeeded him, and governed for a quarter of a century, during which period a large number of buildings were erected, most of which were temples to the gods Siva and Vishnu. Larger armies were conscripted, and an extensive road building programme was launched. He looked out for fresh fields to conquer, and pushed his boundaries westwards. He conquered the independent kingdom of Anindipatura, and established a new capital which he called Isanapura. Throughout his father's reign, he had insisted that the old capital was too close to the eastern frontier, He now decided that with his policy of westward expansion it would be even more remote. Within two years, his territory was extended to the borders of the Mon kingdom of Dvarati.

From the time of his accession, he had been careful to maintain friendly relations with Champa. He had married a lovely Cham princess, and had appointed Cham generals to command his armies. They served him with loyalty and devotion. He unified the kingdom more tightly than had previous kings, but he was arrogant, ambitious, autocratic and ruthless. Much of this attitude can perhaps be excused on account of the unsettled conditions existing at the time. Resolute action was necessary if Chenla was to play the rôle of supreme arbiter in Khmer politics and those of neighbouring states, as he was determined that it should.

Chinese emissaries continued to send their reports to Peking on this progressive and energetic young empire. They were studied with more curiosity than anxiety. "We can always snap if Chenla becomes too ambitious," one shrewd mandarin observed. The emperor's adviser on foreign affairs for the territory which included the Khmer empire is alleged to have shelved the reports with the remark: "Unity is strength. Today, Chenla under Isanavarman possesses it to a remarkable degree, but this scattered empire is a loose confederation which will not submit for long to a central administration which is not yet established, where there are too many cults. Why were they so foolish to move their capital before the old one was consolidated?"

The early Khmer kings left few records, and these were written in Sanskrit and later in Khmer. They developed a liking and skill for carving inscriptions in wood, but over the years these have disappeared. Fortunately, they had considerable skill in working with stone, and a number of stone tablets and columns survived the ravages of time. However, such information as there was available to archaeologists could not be compared for quantity and detail as that amassed by Peking.

These Chinese visitors described the kingdom as rich and prosperous and the people well fed. "They roll up their hair and spend much time washing their bodies and cleaning their teeth with small pieces of poplar." They reported on the manner of their religious devotions, which, because of their diversity, they could not understand.

King Isanavarman came in for considerable comment. To the Chinese visitors he appeared omnipotent, possessing a power and authority which far exceeded that of previous kings. They wrote of him as a "supreme being who received instant obedience akin to adolatry, was not only a ruler but one to whom the highest of all High Priests deferred with abject demeanour".

The skill and ingenuity of the Chenla builders were not lost on the Chinese. They were amazed at the number of temples and large buildings, and they were impressed by the skill and industry of the sculptors, and also their imagination and artistry in decorating some of them with figures of allegorical monsters and deities, and—on a more earthly plane—flowers, trees and animals which were a common daily spectacle. That these buildings were well built is evidence of an acquired knowledge and experience of stresses and strains, for there are still in existence nearly 100 primitive Khmer temples built about this period. Almost all of them are beyond reconstruction, but it is remarkable that with the rough and inadequate tools they were able to construct edifices which lasted so long.

The statues of the gods which were set up inside the temples are generally in a better state of preservation. They are a tribute to the skill, patience and inventive genius of those who worked on them fourteen centuries ago.

The Chenla empire was the forerunner of the great, brilliant and cultured empire of the Khmers. In the early part of the seventh century, the accession of the Tang dynasty in China coincided with a suspension of Cham aggression which was to last until the ninth century. King Indravarman's policy of rapprochement had paid handsome dividends. It is not known whether Chenla had paused to digest its conquests or whether the Tang emperor had lost no time in sending one of the imperial court's polite, double-edged greetings. What is certain is that the Khmers behaved with amazing tolerance towards visitors from other countries, even if they knew them to be spies. They were allowed unrestricted travel, invited to all functions, provided with bodyguards and allowed to talk to all and sundry.

However, Chenla's fortunes rose and fell under successive kings. Some were weak and ineffectual, and the empire passed through periods of crisis when the Khmers were hard pressed by jealous and envious states. One Indianized empire further south had been making a rapid and sustained rise towards supremacy. It was ruled by the Saliendra dynasty or Kings of the Mountains, and the leadership was strong, dynamic and brilliant. Its territory included all modern Sumatra, Java and much of Malaysia.

Chenla maintained an uneasy peace with the new empire, but Saliendra had emerged as the dominant partner. A young king of the Khmers, jealous of the power of the King of the Mountains, and envious of the wealth and luxury of his court, infuriated him by speaking of him in contemptuous terms. This particular king of the Saliendra dynasty, was, according to reports, the Maharaja of Zabag. He was fearless, a wise ruler and a fine seaman. He was convinced that the safety and prosperity of his kingdom depended upon a large fleet of the huge lateen-sailed Arab dhows.

He turned a blind eye to the acts of piracy in which his captains engaged privately, for they had given him proof in abundance of their loyalty; moreover when participating in the more legal affairs of commerce or on the king's business they rendered excellent service.

These dhows were tough, easy to navigate, and capable of fast speeds. They were crewed by tough, resolute sailors who gave no mercy and expected none. Their voyages took them between the ports and cities of Indonesia and Indo-China. They carried cargoes of gold, ivory, precious stones, as well as frankincense and myrrh for use in connection with worship of the god Siva. Probably the cargo which paid the highest dividends dealt in slaves, and girls for the harems.

One of the merchant adventurers who was engaged in this lucrative trade was Sulayman the Merchant, whose name is still a legend. History is indebted to him for an account of the fate of the young Chenla king at the hands of the King of the Mountains.

One day, he was discussing affairs of state with his Chief Minister. His rule had been unsuccessful. He was unpopular, impulsive and reckless, and his oppressive measures had resulted in a long series of civil wars. This long strife had undermined the authority and influence of the Khmers, who up till then had concentrated their power over the lower Mekong region and around the Tonlé Sap. Little had been done throughout his reign for the masses; the power of the court had increased, and the nobility class was more privileged and exclusive than in the past two reigns. The internal unrest had led to the division of Chenla into two separate but vast areas. These were Land Chenla and Water Chenla, or Upper and Lower Chenla. Upper Chenla was the old homeland of the Khmers, and the territory extended to Yunnan. It was more united than the other half and had acquitted itself well in the China wars, particularly against Tongking and Nanchao. Divided Chenla was torn between two hostile factions fighting to place the older lunar dynasty of Anindipatura in a position of unrivalled leadership, and the more recent solar dynasty of Sambhupura challenging its efforts.

In the royal palace, the young king was complaining bitterly of his misfortunes, for which he considered almost everybody responsible but himself. He spoke in envious terms of the kingdom of Zabag, and his fury increased as he compared his lot with that of the Maharajah, King of the Mountain and Lord of the Isles. Suddenly, he shouted at his Chief Minister, a wise and aged counsellor: "I have one desire which I would like to see fulfilled."

"And what is that, Your Majesty?" the counsellor asked.

"I would like to see on a plate before me, the head of the Maharaja of Zabag!"

The counsellor was deeply shocked. Zagab or Java was a powerful kingdom; the Maharajah an autocrat and extremely proud. He gazed around him wildly for a few seconds, and then satisfied that they were alone and had not been overheard, but anxious that the young king would not make further indiscreet utterances in a court riddled with espionage, he implored him to be careful. "I beg of my King never again to express such a wild and intemperate wish. It might be overheard and then the consequences could be disastrous. The people of Zagab and those of our empire have never been opposed to each other either in words or in deeds. Often our two kingdoms have been on the friendliest terms. I urge Your Majesty again, never repeat such words."

The minister's advice had the effect of increasing the king's anger instead of calming him. He was determined to show everyone at court, including the minister, that he was the king-emperor and that his authority was not to be questioned. At a court function, he told his generals and ministers of his desire. The reckless words of the young king soon reached the ears of the Maharajah, who at first would not believe the report. However, he despatched a trusted officer to verify it. When confirmation was received, he called his ministers to a special conference. He was determined that the Chenla king should be punished, for he had made him lose face.

He swore them to secrecy, confided in them his plans, and ordered that 1,000 ships manned by sufficient sailors and soldiers be made ready to sail. He saw to it that news leaked out that the fleet was about to cruise among the many islands of the empire. Thus the Khmer spies in Java were unable to report the true size of the armada or its destination.

After a few days at sea, the fleet met at a pre-arranged rendezvous and sailed to the mouth of the river from which they advanced on the capital by surprise and captured it.

The Maharajah sent messages to the fleeing Khmers, promising to spare their lives. His quarrel, he assured them, was only with their king. Then he seated himself upon the sovereign's chair and waited for the wretched king to be brought before him.

The Maharajah stared at him for some seconds, and then demanded in a loud voice: "What made you express such a foolish wish which you are incapable of fulfilling? It would not have given you happiness even had you been successful, and moreover, what have we done to Chenla that you should wish to see the king of Java dead?"

The helpless king glared furiously at him, but was speechless.

The Javanese king spoke more quietly, but his voice still carried the ring of authority: "You desired to see my head on a plate, but fortunately for Chenla you were not so foolish or evil as to threaten to seize my kingdom and ravage the land. I am going to treat you, therefore, as you threatened to treat me, after which I will return to Zabag without the spoils of war to which I am entitled, but let my clemency serve as a lesson to others who might be tempted to speak or plot as rashly as you. Above all, let not this clemency be misinterpreted." He then signalled to his executioners who forced the king to his knees and struck off his head. He then suitably rewarded the minister who had tried to reason with the king.

The armada lost no time in sailing for home, taking with it the decapitated head of the king. The news of his exploit had reached the Zabag kingdom before the arrival of the armada, and a triumphant welcome awaited the king and his soldiers and sailors. He had the head embalmed, and returned it to Chenla with a further warning to the effect that while he desired peace and friendly relations, he was powerful enough to crush any act of aggression against Saliendra.

Sulayman's narrative ended with the statement that since this tragic incident, the kings of Cambodia every morning on rising, turn their faces towards Zabag and bow in homage to the King of the Mountain and Lord of the Isles.

Historians are vague as to the order of succession to the throne of the Khmer kingdom after the division of Chenla in A.D. 706, but it would appear that the next king of any importance was the dynamic Jayavarman II, who was crowned king in A.D. 802 and founded a dynasty which was to last 600 years.

This amazing king was to unite the Khmers, make Angkor the centre of the kingdom, win independence from Saliendra, and in his reign of forty-eight years make the Khmer empire a powerful and centralized one which was to reach its apogee between A.D. 900 and 1200.

He was to institute the cult of *Devaraja*, which was a new religion or else an adaptation of one which he had studied in Java where he had spent many years. *Devaraja* was the worship of the god-king, and Jayavarman ushered it into his reign with himself as the first of a line of over thirty god-kings who were to rule over the Khmer Empire until its downfall. Jayavarman not only ruled by divine authority. He acquired the power of a deity, to be worshipped and obeyed.

The history of this remarkable empire which at times dominated the entire region, forcing other states into submission, became more colourful and more spectacular with the accession of Jayavarman II. The Khmers were to become more powerful and aggressive than ever. Jayavarman was convinced that complete unity could only be maintained if his subjects looked upon him as a god-king, one to whom they would not only give blind obedience, but would worship. The entire resources of this very rich empire would be devoted to the preservation of the institution of the cult of the god-king. The existence of their king on earth and his identity with the god in his life and the next was to be the predominant reason for living as far as all his subjects, both high-born and low were concerned.

For some five centuries this cult gave the kingdom and its capital a solidarity and a measure of unity unsurpassed in Southeast Asia. It was rarely encountered anywhere else, possibly because it would never have been accepted at its inception. But it was to be embraced freely by the Khmers.

Under Jayavarman II it became a religion, a way of life. It was developed and consolidated by his successors, and made a tremendous impact upon the great Khmer empire. In time it was to lead to its destruction, but before it crashed in ruins, it was responsible for such architectural wonders as Angkor Thom, Angkor Wat, the Bayon, Banteai Srei and other great masterpieces. These were the legacy of the Khmers. The god-kings intended that they should be.

THREE

Capital of Extravagance and Splendour

The symbol of the king's authority was the royal *linga*, the representation of masculine creative power. Here he demonstrated his belief in his identification with the god Siva, for the *linga* had for centuries been sculptured in the form of a phallic image and set up in all places where Siva was worshipped. It symbolized the creative power of the god, and was known as the *Sivalingam*. Under successive kings it had been worshipped in Funan, and when that kingdom was supplanted by Chenla in the leadership of the Khmers, the worship continued. No previous king, however, had presented himself to the people as the re-incarnation of Siva on earth.

In order to consolidate his god-image in the minds of the people, he established what was to become one of the most powerful priest cults in world history. They were dedicated to one purpose, and this was the deification of the king, the worship of the god-king.

Stone was hewn from the vast quarries, the innumerable slaves built temples with incredible speed, driven on by the lash, and to the vast multitudes who came to worship, the priests proclaimed the divine powers and authority of the god-king.

Jayavarman II was king. The word 'varman' originated from Southern India and means 'protector'. He appointed a priest of imposing stature and strong personality as High Priest. This was Sivakaivalya. He was a member of a leading Khmer family. The god-king decreed that this office was to be hereditary, and it remained so for several reigns. Sivakaivalya was ambitious, and possessed of tireless energy. He set about the establishment of a strict hierarchy among his priests. They were placed in categories, and discipline was strict.

The worship of the royal *linga* became at once the official religion. Jayavarman, the first of the god-kings was to make the kingship so absolute that those who followed, automatically assumed the status of gods, and it was accorded them without demur. In the observance of the ritual, symbols and ceremonial of the state religion, the Khmer kings were to emulate a custom which he had instituted in the early years of his reign, which was to build a new holy temple, majestic and beautiful, to house the royal *linga*. And so most of the thirty kings who followed left a monument to commemorate their reign in the form of a massive religious edifice, some of which were of unsurpassed beauty. They were built on the summit of a temple mountain, or if there was no natural hill, an artificial prominence was created. This had to be sited in the centre of the capital which was regarded as the axis of the universe. Some of these sanctuaries are still in a splendid state of preservation and are dealt with in a later chapter.

The Khmer nobility and the wealthy classeses were realists. Within a decade, the cult of the god-king was so strong that they threw in their lot whole-heartedly with their despotic ruler, for he was overcoming all opposition with comparative ease. His proclamation of the cult was an open defiance of Java, for it was a declaration that he recognized no one as his superior on earth. He maintained that he was Chakrayartin, or universal monarch. Zabag—or Java, to give it the more familiar name—decided to ignore the implied challenge.

The effect upon the masses of his military and diplomatic successes was to rally them behind the throne, but, although they were to accept the cult, it met with considerable opposition at first. Jayavarman crushed it with savage cruelty. The cult was established on foundations of oppression, torture, treachery and cunning. He played one prince off against another, planted spies in the homes of those he thought to be against him, and by brilliant propaganda led the masses to believe that their own individual welfare as well as the prosperity of the kingdom depended upon the success of the cult.

He appears to have had difficulty in choosing a site for the new capital, and changed it four times. Although he has gone down in history as the founder of the Angkor kingdom, he was not the founder of the actual city.

He had not forgotten the overwhelming success of the Maharajah of Zabag's surprise attack, the execution of the king and the humiliation of the kingdom. He was loud in his praise of it as a brilliant victory, masterly in its conception, and a triumph of organisation and execution. Key points had been captured, the harbours blocked, escape routes cut off and the army and navy forced to surrender.

The capital had not only to be secure from attack, but must be a city with natural resources, strategically situated and which he could beautify and make worthy of a great empire. His first choice was Indrapura, but after a short stay, he abandoned it and led his army out of the Mekong valley, travelled up its tributary, the Tonlé Sap, and selected a region which became known as Angkor. It was vast and fertile. The lakes and rivers were teeming with fish. Rice would grow in abundance on the plains, for the rainfall was high. He called the actual site for the capital Hariharalaya, or the abode of Harihara. The town is situated south-east of the modern Cambodian town of Siem Reap, which has an airport used by visitors to Angkor Wat today.

After only a brief residence, he made preparations for departure, much to the surprise of his ministers. In actual fact, the kingdom was threatened by rival claimants in both Upper and Lower Chenla. It was a trial of strength, and Jayavarman welcomed it. On his return from the war, in which he achieved an outstanding military success, and treated the defeated armies without mercy, for he was determined that there would be no further attempts, he moved the capital to Amarendrapura. This did not satisfy him, and a further migration took place, this time to Phnom Kulen where he built Mahendrapura. This town was some 30 miles north-east of Angkor.

He quickly realised that his latest choice did not possess the enormous natural advantages of the second site, and this time he moved back permanently to Hariharalaya, which became the capital.

Jean Commaille* asks why the rulers of Angkor installed their capital and the most beautiful of their temples in the region of the great lakes instead of the adjacent mountains. (*"Pourquoi les maîtres d'Angkor ort-ils installé leur capitale et les plus beaux de leurs temples dans la région des grands lacs plutôt que sur les montagnes voisines abondamment pourvues de sources et où leurs citadelles auraient été mieux assises?".*

* Guide aux Ruines d'Angkor, by J. Commaille.

He answers this question by recommending a simple inspection of the site. It provided an inexhaustible supply of fish, which would not only feed the warriors but the innumerable workers, slaves and the vanquished population which the victors maintained to colonise the country; moreover the lakes, which were then much deeper, permitted navigation throughout the year and this facilitated commerce. (*"La réponse est dictée par une simple inspection des lieux . . . le choix de l'endroit permettant de nourrir non seulement les guerriers, mais aussi les innombrables ouvriers, les esclaves et toute la population vaincues que les conquérants gardaient auprès d'eux en vue de coloniser le pays. A cette raison l'on peut ajouter que le lac qui était autrefois beaucoup plus profond qu'aujourd'hui permettait la navigation en toute saison, ce qui facilitait le commerce et l'écroulement des produits d'échange fournis par les régions voisines d'Angkor."*)

Jayavarman built a fortress city on the mountain. It prospered right from the start, for it was fantastically rich in natural resources. He increased the size of his army and navy, for he was determined that weaker territories should either submit to suzerainty or be taken by force. Moreover, he was in urgent need of a large slave army to do the manual work of road-making and quarrying. The capital was close to the huge sandstone quarries of Phnom Kulen, and the slaves would be usefully employed in moving the stone to the different temple sites. Only the lowly peasant stock of the Khmers was employed on such menial work. There was a wide variety of work in higher fields which paid more tempting dividends.

The capital commanded the passes leading to the Korat plateau and the Menam basin. Strategically, it was an excellent springboard for launching campaigns which successive rulers were to conduct against other states.

In A.D. 850 Jayavarman died. A few of the buildings which were his pride and joy are still standing, but they are in such a devastated condition that they are not considered to be worthy of mention among the listed Khmer monuments. However, he will always be remembered as the founder of the great Khmer empire and of its dynasty of god-kings.

His son, Jayavarman III succeeded to the throne and ruled for twenty-five years. He appears to have been content to bask in the glory and achievements bequeathed by his brilliant and gifted father. There is no record of any military successes in his reign.

Perhaps he decided to consolidate his empire's previous victories and gains. It is known that he enjoyed court life and that elephant hunting was his consuming passion. He invented various ingenious contrivances for capturing the huge beasts, and was absent from court for long periods.

Thousands of elephants captured in the jungle were brought back to the capital and trained for war service and ceremonial parades. The *corps d'élite* was the Royal Regiment of Elephants, and there was keen competition for entry into the officers' training school. Jayavarman III strengthened the priestly cult, and increased the already numerous privileges of the aristocracy. He hoped in this way to secure their support in all his undertakings, and also to free himself from as many state duties as possible so that he could spend more time with his chosen comrades hunting elephants. He was an extrovert, and immensely popular with his officers. He met his death in the jungle when he was unable to escape from the charge of a maddened tusker, and the crown passed to his cousin Indravarman I, who reigned from A.D. 887–99.

This remarkable Khmer monarch was deeply and enthusiastically interested in agriculture and building. The population had increased enormously during the past half century, and he realised that more land was needed for rice cultivation, and a water supply which did not entirely depend upon the rains, torrential as they usually were, was also necessary. He had made a careful study of the qualities of the land and had told a Chinese envoy that no country had been more generously endowed by nature with such vital resources. Rich deposits, including iron ore, were found over a wide area. The country was continually flooded with the fertile silt of the mighty Mekong. The rich alluvial plain comprised thousands of acres; the forests abounded in animal life; the rivers were veritable storehouses of fish, for they provided an inexhaustible supply; there was an almost unending amount of sandstone and clay in the Dangrek mountains. The rainfall was enough to satisfy the needs of a much larger population, but too much was allowed to drain away, for the river banks overflowed for long periods. The numerous reservoirs, lakes and ponds which were a feature of the kingdom filled up quickly, as did also the large number of natural hollows.

When Chenla had conquered Funan, the new masters had been

careful to enlist into the services of the administration Funanites of known merit in a wide variety of fields. These included a number of Funanites who were experts in agricultural hydraulics, irrigation and land reclamation. Some of them had invented water machines which were driven by the wind. They were treated as privileged workers and encouraged to experiment on new methods. Indravarman decided to have large barays constructed. These were enormous lakes. He recruited thousands of workers from Funan, and a large number of slaves from all over the empire. He had a complete disregard for their welfare. To him, they were expendable. Consequently, they were given the most strenuous and dangerous tasks, and thousands were drowned in the floods. The barays were not excavated, but formed by building raised dykes. They were filled by the rains, and the rivers whose waters were forced downstream, and so constructed that the water level was above that of the plain. In the dry season, the sluices were opened and the water streamed through the irrigation channels by the force of gravity. It was a simple but ingenius system. The entire rice field area was irrigated by a network of pipe lines and sewers. One baray was over 5 miles long and a mile across.

It was one of the great agricultural advances of the Khmers. Some of these barays are still in a good condition today. Over the years, the system was improved and extended. More advanced water machines were installed. The yield was two and usually three harvests a year. Rice was the basis of the agricultural policy, and one of the chief functions of the different religions was to invoke the assistance of the gods in ensuring the fertility of the soil. In most countries of South-east Asia today, various rites and festivals are held in connection with the rice harvest. They have been handed down through the centuries, and include prayers and thanks to the Earth Goddess.

It is not surprising that with these resources, the country prospered, to become the richest in South-east Asia and the envy of jealous and hostile neighbours. Up and down the rivers and canals, the Khmers transported their merchandise, including the heavy stone for the building of their temples. An excellent network of paved roads put their land communications ahead of other countries.

It is of interest to note that they have always accepted fact and fantasy together. They believed in the existence of a spirit world, of the presence of supernatural beings and their fearsome powers. Festivals and ceremonies were frequently held to propitiate the gods. The principal gods, Siva, Vishnu, and Rama were worshipped. Later, Buddha was to supplant the trinity.

Mass worship, church services as they are understood in the West were not at first a feature of the Khmer religions, although the era of Buddhism was to bring people more closely together in the communal act of prayer, praise and thanksgiving, than the other creeds. The Khmers regarded their temples more as the sanctuaries of the gods, where the image or the royal *linga* was enshrined.

The inscriptions on the columns and walls were mainly concerned with religion and with the king, who, of course, was so closely associated with the god. They were written in Sanskrit.

Indravarman supported the view of the priest-cult that Khmer kings were deities, far above all mortals, and that the priests were serving these gods. The king did not actually inspire the awe and dread in which the numerous gods and spirits were held, nor did he himself endow them with the supernatural powers attributed to them by the masses, but he made no attempt to change in any way these deep-rooted beliefs. Provided that Siva, Vishnu, Brahma and Buddha were accorded their due worship, all were free to indulge their preference for a particular god. Fear of authority, fear of the god-king's miraculous powers, fear of the supernatural—all these were powerful agencies in maintaining discipline over a loosely federated empire.

One general belief was widely accepted by all at this time. It was that the earth was square, an enormous quadrangle encircled by chains of mountains. Beyond these boundaries, unending oceans stretched. In the centre of the quadrangle, Mount Meru soared. Here the gods dwelt. It was the pole of the cosmic forces. There was more than one heaven and more than one hell, all situated above or below the world they lived in. The religions or cults appeared to have at least one common theory which affected all in their lowly state. It was that all life—and this included that of the gods—passed through creation and destruction and reincarnation. The form the reincarnations took depended upon the total good or evil done in previous existences until finally, in Hinduism a state of non-existence or absorption into the bosom of the divine and compassionate *logos* or second person of the trinity; or Nirvana, as in Buddhism, which was the absorption of individuality into the divine spirit, and extinction of all desire and passions.

Indravarman moved the capital of the Khmer kingdom to Roluos. He built Preah Ko, and also the Bakong temple to house the royal *linga*. He also built temples to his parents, thus adhering to the practice of ancestor worship. He instituted the identification of a human being with a god by the combination of the first part of his name and *esvara* for a man and *devi* for a woman. It was during his reign that the stone pyramid originated. This was made up of five superimposed graded terraces, with a temple at the top.

His son, Yasovarman, who succeeded to the throne on his death in A.D. 899 reigned eleven years. In many ways, he was a remarkable man, as well as a great king. Egotistical, extrovert, cultured and ruthless, he dominated the kingdom by the sheer force and brilliance of his own personality, quite apart from the inherited trappings of the god-king. He was a great builder in an extravagance of magnificence. Yasovarman revitalised the Khmer empire.

He was determined that all over the empire he would present an image of a super-being, one who stood apart from previous kings. Adulation from the priestly cult was useful, blind obedience by the courtiers and officials necessary and flattering; loyalty and heroism by the individual soldier essential for the success of his aggressive foreign policy. All acceded to his demands. The counsellors did not wait on him to discuss the great questions of the day. They came to listen and obey. He extended the Khmer empire from the Valley of the Mekong across the Menam Valley to the borders of modern Burma, bringing back huge armies of slaves. He sent his envoys to demand tribute from the kingdom of Malaya.

He saw to it that all were made aware of his outstanding achievements, and that even the humblest citizen would feel pride and joy that he, Yasovarman was their king. Yet even that was not enough. They were to be made to realise that they were living in an age which far outstripped all others in glory and luxury, and that they owed it all to him. Under him, the present Khmer empire had transcended all others in magnificence. Ein Volk! Eine Stimme! Ein Führer! One is tempted to wonder what he would have done with modern propoganda aids, or whether Dr. Goebbels surpassed him in originality and results!

The god Siva dancing

Head of one of the Buddhas at the Bayon

For Yasovarman enrolled an army of artists, poets and sculptors to extol his virtues to the four winds. The poets vied with each other in producing the most sickly eulogy, so pandering to his megalomania. Possibly this king subscribed to the theory that if you told the people the same thing over and over again, they would at some time or other believe it. Inscriptions were inscribed on walls, on columns and on towers.

Some have survived the ravages of time and the elements. None of the Khmer kings suffered from self effacement or modesty. There is no evidence to suggest that they believed that humility was a virtue.

Yasovarman, the "gift of the gods", was "a giant able to wrestle with elephants, and slay tigers with his bare hands". There is no record of his having given a practical demonstration! He was "a unique parcel of splendours whose power was mortal to his enemies". Another inscription which surely brought favour and promotion to the poet and at least a mention to the sculptor, stated that "in observing him, the Creator was amazed and appeared to be saying to himself 'Why did I create a rival for myself in this king?' " And another: "In all the sciences and sports, arts, languages, writings; in dancing, singing and everything else, he was as accomplished as if he had been the Creator of them."

Students of Khmer civilisation, commenting on these inscriptions, argue that the Khmers were not the most literary of the Indianized states and that they have left no literature to posterity. The expressions and the verses were influenced by Indianized origins. Poetry, songs and speeches had one main theme, which was praise of the god-king, and this stultified both originality and style.

The priests accepted usurpers to the throne without resistance, and duly consecrated them. In this way they ensured the permanence of their own powerful position in the kingdom. Their efforts to make Yasovarman appear omnipotent were crowned with success. It was believed that he interceded with the spirits, placated the evil genii and invoked the power of the rain gods to fill the reservoirs with the life-giving water for the rice fields. Cambodia has always had more than an adequate supply of rain, but the bountiful supply which lashed down on her land year after year was no doubt laid to the credit of the gods.

However, Yasovarman was an outstanding king. He built with

4

an imagination, a splendour and on a scale which had not been seen before. After ruling from his capital at Hariharalaya for a few years, he set about constructing a new one. It was built with fantastic speed. The wretched slaves perished in their thousands. From a seemingly unending supply their ranks were filled, only to be depleted again, but Yasodharapura, a fabulous new capital was completed and named after him. It was a city of splendour and colour, the first city of Angkor, and stretched over 10 miles. Slaves were put to work in different sectors, excavating and building. It was laid out compactly and elegantly. If Yasovarman really conceived it, then he ranks among the great architects of the Khmers. However, with his uncanny flair for picking the right man, it is more likely that it was the work of artists and architects endowed with a most vivid imagination, and visionaries with a boldness which must have been infectious. A moat over 200 yards wide encircled this exciting city.

Yasovarman built his capital around a natural hill named Phnom Bakheng, which he had selected as the centre of his "mighty and terrible city". He dedicated it to Siva. He was obsessed with this god, and this consuming passion was maintained until his death. He ordered that its images be built all over the kingdom. The worship of Siva was more fashionable than at any other period in Cambodian history. Wherever the traveller journeyed, the ubiquitious Siva frowned down on him.

The new capital proved to be a most popular choice with the Khmers. Phnom Bakheng, a high hill was a natural choice and an ideal setting for the temple mountain, for it represented the Golden Meru, the centre of the world of cosmology. The creative powers of the universe were concentrated there, and it was believed that a symbolic staircase led from the mountain to heaven. Yasovarman rebuilt the hill to form five terraces, which he faced with masonry. On the summit five sandstone towers were erected, the central one housing the royal *linga*, Yasodharesva.

As the hill represented Mount Meru, Yasovarman considered that the Siem Reap river represented the sacred Ganges. He changed its course so that it could help to support the new capital, and built the huge reservoir called the East Baray to provide an adequate supply of water. Around the base of the sacred hill, nearly 1,000 artificial ornamental ponds were constructed in a geometrical pattern. They served as natural mirrors for the architectural gems nearby.

His passion for building increased as his reign continued. Many noble edifices were built. One beautiful temple, the Preah Viharn, crowned a triangular headland 1,600 feet above the plain, and was still in an excellent state of preservation several centuries later, when it was judged to be one of the outstanding masterpieces of Khmer architecture.*

Almost every hill in the Khmer capital and many outside it were crowned with a shrine. Siva was paramount, and Yasovarman built monasteries to increase the priest population. Yet this tireless monarch did not limit his activities to war, and building temples to Siva. He modernised the irrigation canals and put more land down to rice cultivation. When he died in A.D. 900 Cambodia, the Khmer empire, was rich, powerful and prosperous. Its territory stretched to China in the north, Champa in the east, the Indian Ocean in the west, with northern Malay included.

The next two kings were his sons. They were followed by a usurper who took the title of Jayavarman IV and set up a new capital at Koh Ker, but it was short lived. None of these kings, nor the usurper's son have any claim to history. The next one to rule over the Khmers was Rajendravarman II, who reigned from A.D. 944–68. He transferred the capital back to Angkor, and it remained the royal city for nearly 500 years, until it was abandoned in A.D. 1432.

He launched an extensive building programme, and managed to keep Cambodia out of wars after a successful invasion of Champa in the first year of his reign not only secured his frontiers but gave him more slaves and rich treasures. In over twenty years peace he built many temples including the beautiful Banteai Srei. One of the celebrated inscriptions recording the outstanding gifts and virtues of the Khmer kings tells us that this one "restored the sacred city of Yasodharapura, deserted for so long, and built three

---

* In 1958 Cambodia and Thailand contested the ownership of this temple, and there were angry demonstrations in both capitals. The author watched the processions in Bangkok. The dispute was passed to the United Nations, who adjudicated in favour of Cambodia. The temple was situated very close to the frontier but inside Cambodian territory. Feeling ran high in Thailand, but Field-Marshal Sarit, as Head of State, succeeded in calming his countrymen, pointing out that, as members of the U.N., they should accept its decisions.

houses ornamented with shining gold, and palaces glittering with precious stones like the palace of Mahendra on earth".

His son, Jayavarman V, succeeded him. He was a scholar, and during his reign the capital entered on an era of culture and learning. Architects, poets, musicians and dancers flocked to the capital. Women enjoyed a period of emancipation, and a few were admitted to the Privy Council which existed at that time. Leading Brahman families were appointed to high office, and they selected their friends to work under them, or for employment in other fields. The result was that Brahman influence during this reign was extensive. Brahman astrologers were held in high esteem.

He reigned for thirty-three years, and, although he was a man of peace and had pursued a pacifist policy throughout his reign, the royal propagandists gave him a warrior image which must have caused eyebrows to rise in court circles and created terror in the hearts of envoys from other countries. One inscription stated that "when he sets out to march, the earth with its mountains is agitated as the sea is disturbed by a tempest, by the shock of his armies . . . . He strikes terror in his enemies. When, in his anger, his lion roar was heard, enemy kings fled to the depths and safety of the forest."

Poor Jayavarman V! He wanted peace and tranquillity, to be surrounded by his artists and musicians and to watch his exquisite Phimeanakas taking shape.

The next king reigned for forty-eight years. This was Suryavarman I. The era of peace which had lasted some sixty years practically disappeared overnight. In the year which had passed since the death of Jayavarman, two kings had reigned for only a few months and are of no account.

Suryavarman's reign was born in war. A usurper to the throne of the Khmers, he led an army of invasion from Malaya, penetrated deep into Khmer territory, set up petty principalities with puppet rulers, and recruited large numbers of mercenaries and slaves. Within a few months, his position was so strong that resistance began to crumble. He won a succession of lightning victories with such ease that he was regarded as being invincible. One can imagine the flatterers at court already writing out the inscriptions, and the sculptors preparing the stones! But Suryavarman himself was providing the inspirations. Some at least of the praises were already richly deserved. And when the capital opened its gates to his victorious armies, the priest-cult and the nobles lost no time in acclaiming as their king one of the most dynamic personalities ever to rule over the vast empire.

He conducted the affairs of the kingdom from a position of unrivalled authority. His victorious advances had made him something of a legend. There were no minor insurrections to detract his attention from the main task of strengthening the empire. He led his armies in a brilliant campaign against Siam, and after this country had been conquered, Cambodia enjoyed a long period of peace. Suryavarman had more buildings constructed, but concentrated on making the capital more majestic. The temple of Takeo, the first Khmer temple to be built of sandstone, was erected during his reign, and more irrigation works constructed outside the city.

Buddhism, which had been practised side by side with the Siva-Vishnu-Rama trinity, slowly began to increase its influence over the people. There is no evidence of any opposition from the priests of the Hindu trinity, nor of any unusual activity on the part of the Buddhist monks. The wave appears to have been spontaneous from the ordinary people. Statues of the Buddha, the Enlightened One, were placed in temples to the trinity and all were worshipped together.

He planned the famous Grand Plaza, with its majestic towers which were intended to soar above all other buildings, and the Royal Enclosure. The work was far from complete when he died, but he left the capital an even more beautiful and majestic city than when he had made his triumphant entry to take over the throne of the Khmers.

His son Udayadityavarman succeeded him. He was to prove a weak and ineffectual monarch, but the scribes, poets and sculptors all joined forces to produce in stone the usual propaganda. The cult of the god-king had to be maintained. However, one is tempted to wonder whether they had their tongues in their cheeks in connection with one particular inscription which tells us that he was a "prince of great energy who excelled in seducing women to his will by his beauty, warriors by his bravery, the learned by his good qualities, the people by his power, and Brahmans by his charity". They were certainly recording at least one truth, for this gift of the gods appears to have been more obsessed with women than with Siva. His sexual prowess must have been remarkable.

It is possible that in his preoccupation with this activity, affairs of state were allowed to drift.

The strong resolute rule of his father had given discipline and leadership to the nation, but these qualities deteriorated rapidly under a weak and vacillating king who was such a striking and pitiful contrast. Minor revolts broke out; there was a mutiny among the slaves which was suppressed with ferocious cruelty. Udayadityavarman entrusted the defence of the kingdom to a tough young general called Sangrama, but he could not defend it on all fronts, and the soldiers had lost much of their enthusiasm for campaigns too far from their homes. King Anawrahta of Pagan subdued the Mons of southern Burma, and captured their capital, Thaton. This reverse inspired the dissident factions among the Khmers to open revolt. One of the king's own generals rallied his supporters in the north-west and marched on the capital. Sangrama defeated the rebels, and then was forced to defend the capital from another attack which came from the east.

On all fronts the king blundered. There were several minor rebellions in the capital, which were evidence of the general discontent existing in the kingdom. Most of them had a religious background, and this was most unusual in a country remarkable for its tolerance. Udayadityavarman endeavoured to make Saivism the official religion of the kingdom, to the exclusion of other cults and creeds. He did not openly oppose Buddhism but he discouraged its adoption at court, treated the saffron-robed monks with indifference and built temples only to Siva. The Buddhists had been treated with generosity by his father, and during his reign their numbers had shown a marked increase. Their disappointment at his son's attitude changed to anger. It is of interest to note that this was directed against the king and his officials. Relations between the worshippers of the trinity and Buddha remained amazingly calm.

He built the Baphuon, an enormous gilded temple, but its purpose was not so much to beautify the capital or provide an additional place of worship for the people, but to house his *linga*, which was of gold, and to be his burial place. And under the protection of the all powerful Siva in life he hoped for compassion in death. This temple is his only claim to fame, but it is considered by many to be the most perfect specimen of Khmer art.

Udayadityavarman left the kingdom seething with unrest on

his death in A.D. 1065. This unhappy state of affairs continued throughout the reigns of the next three kings. These were Harshavarman III, the former king's younger brother, who was crowned in A.D. 1066 and who made a desperate effort to restore peace to the divided kingdom, but whose methods were not sufficiently resolute to meet the demands of rival factions. Civil war broke out. After fourteen years, the king lost his throne to another. This was Jayavarman VI, who fared no better. The kingdom was partitioned, for the family of the former king led a revolt in the south. The next king, Dharanindravarman I, was already an elderly man when he ascended the throne in A.D. 1107 and great things were expected of him. He had spent several years in a monastery and was renowned for his piety and kindness. Unfortunately, he did not realise that what was needed was strong, determined action to suppress the revolts and punish the leaders, including rival claimants to the throne. His policy of appeasement and concessions was ruinous. The sculptors were busy with their chisels. Inscriptions told of his talents and virtues, but six years later they were forced to start work in preparing others to a new king.

This was his nephew who deposed him, led a lightning campaign against the armies of the former king Harshavarman, overwhelmed them and ruthlessly suppressed other outbreaks, and had himself proclaimed Suryavarman II at Angkor in A.D. 1113. He has gone down in history as one of the four great kings of the Khmers. Some historians regard him as the greatest. He was to reign for thirty-seven years, during which time he was to give the world its greatest Khmer masterpiece, the magnificent Angkor Wat, and the best preserved of all Khmer buildings. Cambodia is famous for its legends, and one of them states that Angkor Wat was not built by human hand but by the god Indra, who came down to earth to build it.

Another declares that it was constructed by the gods, who then departed to the Land of Eternal Happiness where they look down from the skies.

What is certain is that it is the largest religious building in the world, bigger than Vatican city. It took just over forty years to build.

Suryavarman regarded himself as the re-incarnation of Vishnu. Vaisnavism flourished more vigorously during his reign than in

any other. Angkor Wat was built not so much as a place of worship in life, but as his mausoleum at death. From the commencement of his reign he had a pre-occupation with death, which
persisted until it overtook him. The central shrine of Angkor Wat
—the word *wat* means temple—housed a gold statue of Vishnu
mounted on a *garuda*, which on festival occasions and special
religious ceremonies was taken out of the shrine. The statue was a
representation of the king deified as Vishnu.

Most entrances to this fabulous temple faced east. The main
entrance faced west, in the direction of the dead. It was in keeping
with the Khmer aspect of a tomb, and was a classic example of
the temple mountain and the centre of the kingdom. Here Suryavarman was united in death with Vishnu as he had been in life.

He gave Cambodia greatness on an unparalleled scale. Khmer
civilisation reached its height. In the first half of his reign the
empire prospered and was very rich. Suryavarman was to leave it
impoverished by his extravagance.

His sweeping, speedy victories over the dissident elements
within the empire during the first decade of his reign encouraged
him to pursue a most aggressive foreign policy, where the extension of the empire was a motive which was secondary to his own
self aggrandisement. The bas-reliefs at Angkor Wat were to
display to posterity his military and naval triumphs. The two
principal motifs were the god-king, who far excelled all previous
kings in god-like attributes, and the glorification of war.

Most of the bas-reliefs among the Khmer monuments depicted
a religious scene, but here we have several representing triumphant
parades of Suryavarman's infantry and cavalry—one over 100
yards long, where the smart bearing of the Khmer soldiers contrasts with the slovenly turn-out of her Siamese allies—a naval
pageant and a huge battle scene between the Khmers and Chams.
The victory parades were not lacking in detail. There were banners and military bands.

Here, at Angkor Wat, where foreign envoys came to gape in
amazement, the élite of the land were provided with gala representations in stone of their wonderful king. But all could not
come to the capital, and so the sculptors took the tools of their
trade to the provinces and inscribed columns and pillars to the
Greatest of the Khmers, "one for whom there was no rival".

However, he gradually became disillusioned with his foreign

campaigns. His armies ravaged Champa and followed the retreating forces into Annam. The king of Champa made an alliance with Annam, whereupon Suryavarman invaded Champa, occupied the capital of Vijaya and took over the kingdom. The Chams fought back so stubbornly that the Khmers made a partial retreat, but North Champa remained under Khmer domination for the next thirty years. The king of Champa fled the country and died in exile. The Chams never forgave the Khmers. They reproached Suryavarman for having made a pact with them against the Annamite kingdom of Dai-Viet, the term for the modern Vietnam, and then turning against them. The army of occupation, which the Khmers left behind them in North Champa, soon realised that they were in enemy country. Eyes burning with hatred glared at them defiantly wherever they went, and those soldiers who left the barracks in only small parties were fortunate if they returned alive.

Suryavarman's armies went on to penetrate deep into the Golden Peninsula, and occupied the Mon kingdom. Brilliant and colourful victory parades were held in Angkor. However, he had little peace from the renewed uprisings in Champa, and his troops met with little success in Annam. He was a realist and he accepted the situation. The country was not enthusiastic about his campaigns. It had been some years since the Khmer armies had brought back the rich fruits of victory. He decided to consolidate the gains he had made in the early years of his reign until he was ready to invade Tongking, and in the meantime he extended his already extensive building programme.

He created more princes and nobles, with the result that there was an even larger ruling class which was very rich through corruption and the exploitation of the slaves, and possessed privileges no other section of the community ever hoped to acquire.

Angkor was a dream city where banqueting and revelry were nightly affairs. Drug taking was common. Opium does not appear to have been used on a large scale, except among court circles. The only evidence concerning its early use is that it was among the drugs administered as medicine. The Khmers experimented with roots and flowers, and it is quite likely that they stumbled on it by accident, in which case it was taken in a primitive form then later processed to become more refined.

It was obtained from the unripe head of the poppy, the seed capsule of the flower, which yields a juice which today is dried to become the opium of commerce, although it is not generally employed medicinally. However, the existence of the drug was well known. Chinese scholars had established that it originated in the eastern Mediterranean. The poppy was used by the ancient Greeks. Dioscorides, in the first century after Christ, gave an accurate description of opium as we know it today. It was included among the herb lists of the Assyrians. Its culture spread slowly east, but the Chinese were well aware of its properties in the seventh century. It has always been found in the Shan States, Burma and Siam, where it has grown in a prolific, semi-wild state, and where the main supply is to be found today.

The chief narcotic drugs were derived from rice and certain roots which were very potent and addictive and obtained without much difficulty. They were an additional diversion for the court circles, and a pleasant form of oblivion for the half starved and overworked.

Every sort of vice was practised in his illustrious capital, but life was geared to the distractions of the aristocracy who presented a united front. They built sanctuaries and shrines identifying themselves with this or that particular god, and serving as their mausoleums when they died. They vied with each other to produce the most exquisite shrine. The skilled craftsman was at a premium, his place in society high. Lovely ladies of the court conferred their favours freely upon sculptors of renown, who already had enough of the earth's goods, but could be seduced into their service.

Stupas sprang up all over the capital, and proud princes displayed their latest acquisition to an admiring and often envious party. The artistic talent of the Khmers was revealed in Suryavarman's reign as in no other, but it was all devoted to the construction of religious buildings. Vishnu was now at the zenith of his popularity.

The slaves struggled to lift the massive stones into position so that the sculptors could work on them. The pitiful, half starved creatures were thrashed, tortured, killed or died from exhaustion. A cry of anguish went up from scores of thousands of these miserable creatures. It went unheeded, but they were plotting. All that mattered to the ruling classes was that they were building a magnificent capital which would be the envy of the countries of South-east Asia. Visitors flocked to it from all over the region. A large number came from China, with which country Survavarman had pulled off a diplomatic triumph for which the highest praises had been sung at court and recorded in stone.

His approach to the emperor had met with a cordiality far beyond his expectations. He had been invited to send an embassy. It was received with much ceremony and courtesy. Later, two more were sent. He was the first Khmer king for 300 years to establish diplomatic relations. On the occasion of the third embassy, the emperor awarded him high honours and gave him expensive presents. Commercial treaties were exchanged to the advantage of both empires.

About A.D. 1149 he launched an attack on Tongking, but the leadership was ineffectual, the preparations had been inadequate and the war was unpopular with the powerful aristocratic class. Angkor was rapidly becoming a Babylon of idolatory, luxury and ease. The officers grumbled at being called away from the capital. The Khmer armies were hurled back with ignominy into their own territory. He died the following year.

There was much mourning over the passing of this brilliant ruler, but when the ministers began to take stock of the nation's economy they found that the country was in a desperate plight. The king had spent with an extravagance which far exceeded that of the aggregate of the past four reigns. Angkor Wat was a unique edifice. Today it is still one of the most noble religious buildings in the world, but it had been built at an astronomical cost. This was not all. Too many temples had been erected, and a large number had been ornamented with gold. silver and precious stones. It was a deeply religious period, when the king's crusade to build temples to his god had been supported by so many at an appalling cost, for the resources of the kingdom had been severely taxed.

He had also imbued them with a deep national pride, which was to remain with them long after his death, and which was to be revived over and over again—if at times without the desired result—down through the years. He had given the kingdom the magnificent, awe-inspiring Grand Plaza and Royal Enclosure. His namesake and predecessor had inspired it, but it was this king who had built it, and on a far more grandiose scale than had been intended. With its imposing, broad avenues and stately towers, it enhanced the beauty of the capital. It was the great square of the Khmers, where the pageant of life unfolded, and was often the scene of great pageantry and victory celebrations.

Eight hundred years later, the Young Nationalists of Cambodia spoke and wrote of it with pride. They were the descendants of the Khmers who had built it. Suryavarman II had written his name large in the annals of Khmer history.

FOUR

God-Kings of Angkor

The slaves were in a mutinous state, and another hostile faction consisted of young men of the intellectual class who were embittered by the nepotism which kept them out of the higher fields of employment for which their abilities were more than adequate.

In the provinces, the outcry that their towns and roads had been neglected in order that Angkor could emerge as the wonder city could not be silenced. Once again the proud empire was in the throes of internal unrest.

A slow but inexorable wave of revulsion against this ostentatious and blatant worship of the gods began to move over the kingdom. The ruling classes, the priest cult and those who were vociferous in their support of the *Devaraja* or the cult of the god-king were quick to recognise the symptoms, but believed that it was only a temporary agitation. After all, they argued, Angkor Wat would not require much more expenditure. They could pacify the provinces, build the roads for which the governors had petitioned over the years. But it was not as simple as that. Buddhism with its simplicity and tolerance was spreading over the kingdom. Then the king who succeeded him, Dharanindravarman II, was a Buddhist. This was a departure from the long-established trinity, and it was a setback for the followers of the *Devaraja*. The priest cult had great difficulty in reconciling the long practice and all the paraphernalia of the cult of the god-king with the simplicity which the new king endeavoured to introduce into his reign.

More Buddhists made the voyage from India, sure of a friendly welcome. The simple Buddhist temples increased in number. However, internal unrest was only just below the surface. The Khmers were bankrupt. The fruits of this rich and fertile land—its crops, minerals and precious stones—had been employed in building great religious buildings, when at least a portion should

have gone towards producing more goods for export and barter-
ing for imports which were vital to balance the budget.

The Buddhist king died after a rule of ten years. Very little
building had been carried out beyond additions to Angkor Wat.
He had kept the country at peace with neighbouring states and
there was a slight improvement in its economic position, but the
reign had not been sufficiently spectacular for the privileged
classes. They were determined that, come what may, their illustrious capital must be even more majestic and beautiful. Treasures
and ornaments had to be brought in from China and India, but
under Suryavarman the ship building programme had slowed
down. At that time a considerable amount of the work in the
temples was of wood construction. The Khmers were renowned
for their wood carving. It is unfortunate that over the centuries
it disintegrated and was lost to posterity, leaving only the stone,
for it was used for the ceilings, doors, floors and furniture of the
temples. There was a heavy demand not only for the wood but
for craftsmen able to fashion it. The Khmer shipyards were
accordingly denuded of timber and craftsmen. Temple building
was top priority.

Jayavarman, his son, should have succeeded him, but he, too,
was a Buddhist and a very devout one. He knew that he was not
wanted by the war lords and that his accession would spark off
the smouldering fires of civil war. Bloodshed was contrary to
Buddhist teaching, and rather than divide the kingdom, he went
into exile in Champa. It was an odd choice for a sanctuary.
Champa was preparing for a war of revenge against Cambodia,
although the Khmers awaited it with lofty disdain. They were
convinced that they were more than a match for the Chams, for
only a few years ago, under Suryavarman the Great, they had
beaten them. The Khmers drew strength and confidence from
their awe-inspiring capital.

Yasovarman II, another of his sons, became king. He was to rule
only five years. He was killed in the savage fighting of the civil
war which finally overwhelmed the capital, but before he met his
death, he had to deal with a peasants' revolt which appears to have
started in the provinces. Resentment against the hardships they
had been forced to endure under Suryavarman, and the failure of
the new kings to alleviate their sufferings were the main causes.

The uprising was spontaneous. Peasants and slaves seem to have combined in an attempt to rid themselves of the tyrannical system and the cruelty of the officials. It started with the murder of a few of the king's tax collectors. Of course, the slaves had ringleaders, and their amazing successes of the first few weeks inspired them to advance on the capital. There was actually some sporadic fighting within the city walls.

The court was at first astounded, then furious. This was the first time that the slaves and peasants had dared to come out in open rebellion against authority. It was not only a defiance of the court, it was an insult to the *Devaraja*. The well-trained, well-fed royal troops went into action with a zest and ruthlessness which showed the contempt the master race felt towards those of low birth or caste. They hunted the desperate men and women across the fields, they rode them down in the roads, they manned their fast ships and pursued them up and down the canals. This was a new sport for those seeking new distractions at court. Hunt the slaves! Against the well-organized and disciplined forces they had no chance. The revolt was crushed with unprecedented harshness. Indeed so ferocious were the captors in their treatment of the prisoners that one must assume that they were determined to strike terror into the hearts of the slave and peasant population, and deter them from any future attacks.

The chief ministers were shrewd enough to realise that if the wholesale massacre by the soldiers did not stop, the labour force would be reduced to the point where it could create a problem. The rebellious condition of the kingdom did not encourage the army chiefs to send out raiding parties to bring back slaves from over the borders.

Accordingly, in the presence of the miserable wretches who packed the vast field, the ringleaders were dragged to a huge trench which they had been forced to dig. There they were thrown in, and buried alive. A large number of their followers were dragged up to an improvised platform so that all could see them, and their hands or fingers and toes amputated. Some had their noses cut off. They were the slaves and peasants who had been captured in the capital. This punishment was intended to make them marked men for life.

For the next few months, the peasants and slaves went about their work silently. Silence descended upon the usually animated capital, but it was the silence of the grave. The vanquished were cowed, at least temporarily, but there was an air of uneasiness at court, a feeling that the punishment had been too severe, a fear that there could well be another uprising, as indeed there was to be.

However, this mood at the court soon passed. There were distractions, in plenty. For the nobles and the wealthy there was a continual round of pleasure, and the revolt was forgotten; but in the rice fields and bamboo huts, in the houses of their masters, the slaves continued to plot. The wretched conditions under which they lived made their lives of little consequence to themselves.

The peace at court which followed the suppression of the revolt was only brief. Within a year the kingdom was once again plunged in civil war. A rival claimant, who possessed the lengthy name of Tribhuvanandityavarman, made a bid for the throne. Not for him the support of the ill-disciplined slaves and peasants with their antiquated weapons. He appealed to those disgruntled members of the aristocracy, which gave him a measure of palace backing. He appealed to the young intelligentsia who had been kept out of office by palace favourites. There were a large number of capable youths who were opposed to the hierarchies which pervaded Khmer society. Finally there were the ambitious, frustrated officers. Many of them, particularly the young intelligentsia, had been deeply moved by the desperate courage of the half-naked sub-humans, as they were looked upon at court. Some were ashamed at the passive part they themselves had played in the insurrection. Favouritism and hereditary appointments were their main grievances. They listened to the would-be usurper. The man with the name struck and carried all before him. Yasovarman was killed. In neighbouring Champa, his brother Jayavarman heard the news of the ambitious usurper's treachery, and dashed back to Angkor, either to help him or to seize the throne for himself. When he arrived, the revolution was over and the usurper was on the throne. Jayavarman, true to his Buddhist principles, refused to lead a counter revolt and again retired to Champa.

Tribhuvanandityavarman wasted little time on the disaffected officers, young aristocrats and intellectuals. The ruling class had to present a united front. He acted ruthlessly. A few mass public executions or exile to the outlying provinces and their active resistance was over, but they continued to plot and stir up opposition.

The lotus bud towers of Angkor Wat as seen from the air

Angkor Wat: the causeway and *naga* balustrade with multi-headed cobra. (*left*) Group of temple dancers from a bas-relief in the inner courtyard of Angkor Wat

With Angkor still reeling from the shock of civil war, Champa struck. The Cham spies had reported that the kingdom was more divided than it had been for the past twenty years; the defences were weak, the customary vigilance of the frontier troops had given place to apathy. The new king was making desperate efforts to consolidate his position as god-king, the priest-cult and the court were rallying to his aid, but unity was a long way off. Jaya Indravarman IV, King of Champa, sent envoys to Annam, charged with a secret mission. It was to solicit that kingdom's neutrality in the impending war against Cambodia. His request was granted and he began his preparations. In A.D. 1170 he ordered his armies to invade the country. In an all-out attack in which his well-trained calvalry advanced over the frontier, destroying the crops and burning the villages, he stormed on to Angkor.

The Chams had perfected a weapon of warfare which the Khmers did not possess. This was the crossbow. Their marksmen inflicted fearful slaughter on the Khmer soldiers and soon demoralized them. Tribhuvanandityavarman was nothing if not a leader, and a very courageous one at that. He stormed at his men, inspired them with confidence and ordered the famous Royal Regiment of Elephants into the defence. These mobile war machines saved the day. The Chams had been promised the rich prize of Angkor, or as they still called it Yasodharapura, with loot and women in abundance, and they fought with reckless courage to storm the earth defences and risk a fearful death in the crocodile infested moats to gain the golden city. The attempt at invasion failed. Tribhuvanandityavarman's elephants and cavalry thundered after the fleeing Chams, trampling the dead and dying in the bloody carnage of the battlefield, while the crocodiles, those fearsome guardians of the capital, continued their grisly feast.

Jayavarman escaped with the retreating Chams. He had expectations that in the event of a Cham victory the Khmer king would be deposed and that he would replace the usurper. Apparently this was not at variance with his Buddhist principles as he would not in this way have come by the crown through civil war, but by the defeat of foreign aggression.

The kingdom of Champa licked its wounds, but went ahead with plans for a further invasion. The Khmers were over-confident. They believed that the losses the Chams had sustained in men and horses were so appalling that they would never again commit a hostile act against Cambodia. The Chams realised that an attack by land had little chance of success. Their cavalry was too weak and it would be many years before it was up to the required strength. They placed great reliance upon massive cavalry charges. Their spies suggested to Jaya Indravarman IV that a landing by sea could well be successful. The king was impressed with the details of the plan they had worked out, and gave orders for a large number of ships to be built in different shipyards. Success depended upon secrecy and the element of surprise.

In 1177 the fleet sailed. It proceeded to the Mekong delta, then up the river to Angkor. The success of the plan far exceeded Jaya Indravarman's wildest hopes. The soldiers and sailors laughed exultantly when they saw the quays deserted, and jumping from their ships, they poured into the streets of the Golden City. Screaming blood curdling war cries to terrify the bewildered townspeople, they struck them down as they dashed from their houses to find out what had caused the sudden commotion. Few of the defenders had time to seize a weapon and defend life and property before they died under the blows of the frenzied hordes. The Chams worked to a well-rehearsed plan. They captured the royal arsenal, the harbours, the barracks, ministries and all key places. They violated the sacred temples, smashed the sanctuaries, defiled the gods and stabbed or throttled the priests.

Surprise and speed had brought them complete victory. The wooden barriers and earthworks which were the Khmers' lines of defence were quite inadequate to meet the furious onslaught of the Chams. Their light, portable planks had bridged the moats. Battering rams and catapults inflicted fearful damage. The Cham king had looked upon the campaign as a crusade. There was to be no middle way. It could not be otherwise. Total annihilation for them if they were seen approaching Angkor, or a victory which would be remembered throughout their history if the Khmers were caught napping.

The Cham officers put their men in position to prevent the Khmers from linking up, and also to cut off their retreat. King Tribhuvanandityavarman had usurped the throne, and in so doing had made many enemies. But on that day, he proved himself a leader and a hero. He rallied his troops and led one counter attack after another until he was hurled from his war elephant to die from innumerable stab wounds. The Emperor of the Khmers had been slain. The cry went up all over the capital, and all resistance crumbled. Mighty Angkor, for 300 years the capital of a vast empire, cradle of Khmer greatness, had fallen to a surprise attack in a day or so.

It was the greatest disaster which had overwhelmed the Khmers since that day, 350 years back when the King of the Mountains had sailed his fleet into Chenla and beheaded its ruler, the young and impetuous king.

The Chams determined to humiliate the proud Khmers. The capital was given over to an orgy of murder, destruction, burning and rape. No one was immune; the ladies of the court were singled out, possibly because of their light skins, beauty and also the shame of being raped by a common soldier. Priceless treasures were torn from the temple walls and sanctuaries; precious stones, gold, jewellery and regalia. This continued for several days. The loot was loaded on ships to be taken back to Champa. To deepen the humiliation, a large number of Khmer ships were used to tranship their own treasures. Great numbers of Khmers were roped together and transported to Champa to be driven on by blows through the streets of the capital in a victory procession. The tables had indeed been turned on the Khmers, for it had been their policy during the past four centuries and more to bring back thousands of prisoners and parade them past the victory columns.

When at last the order was given to make ready for departure, the Cham forces, red-eyed and exhausted after their sexual excesses, sailed for home, leaving behind a stunned and crushed city, with an army of occupation to keep them in a state of subjugation.

Throughout the empire, the news of the lightning collapse was received with consternation. The repercussions were tremendous. Hostile states began to ponder over the much boasted invincibility of Angkor. Was it all a myth? What was wrong with the government that such a catastrophe could have occurred? Some states withheld the payment of the annual tribute. Khmer envoys to foreign capitals were quick to notice a falling off in the courtesies and lavish receptions to which they had been accustomed and taken as a right over the years.

The Siamese had infiltrated into the Menam Valley and had settled in Louvo or Lopburi, as it is known today. They were a warlike race, and had already established a remarkable measure of unity. They seized their opportunity and sent a mission to China. This was an open gesture of defiance of Khmer authority.

Jayavarman returned to Cambodia. It is very probable that the Chams placed no restrictions on his departure, hoping that he would rule over a defeated kingdom as a puppet of Champa. He was shocked at the sight of his devastated and pillaged capital. Only the stone buildings had escaped the holocaust which had raged through Angkor, destroying everything else. Most of the records had gone up in flames, for they were inscribed on palm leaves or on wood. He found a cowed population which greeted him apathetically.

Jayavarman launched an all-out drive to chase the Chams out of the country and to carry the war into their territory. The Brahman priests crowned him Jayavarman VII, and he was to go down in history as the greatest of the Khmer emperors. At first. the court circle and the army chiefs were amazed at his tireless energy and his thirst for revenge on the Chams. All had known him as a devout Buddhist, but if bloodshed was against the teachings of the Enlightened One whose principles he had practised for so long—he was now 50—he decided to forget about them, at least for the time being. The Chams were hated with savage intensity. A rallying call to make war on them united the kingdom.

He made his preparations with great care. Land and sea forces would attack Champa. He had the Royal Regiment of Elephants trained and placed on a war footing. Angkor was inspired. The impending war was looked upon as a crusade. Jayavarman carried all before him. It was a crushing defeat for the Chams on land and sea, and he was to commemorate it by an enormous bas-relief sculptured on the walls of the Bayon—which was his own funerary monument—and also on the walls of Banteai Chmar. The capital was sacked, the king taken prisoner. The Chams had been ruthless in their treatment of the Khmers. They were to find the Khmers just as merciless. Jayavarman's armies overran Champa. The terrifying charges of the elephants demoralized the defenders who turned and fled, but those who could not were massacred on the spot. The aged and infants were mowed down. Khmer armies swept through Champa like a raging, tornado killing and burning. In the end, scores of thousands of the able bodied were driven back to Angkor, but those judged incapable of carrying out the arduous work which awaited them were butchered with callous indifference.

When finally the Khmer hordes withdrew, Champa was one huge devastated area; its cities and villages wiped out. His revenge was not complete. The Chams had destroyed his magnificent capital; therefore they should help to rebuild it. Large numbers, driven on by the whips of the merciless overseers hewed out the sandstone and laterite, repaired the temples, replaced the ornaments they had stolen, and added those which Jayavarman had collected by way of an indemnity. The captured soldiers were enrolled in Khmer regiments under the command of Khmer officers and were sent off to the wars.

Victory parades went on continuously for some days. Kings of states which paid allegiance to Cambodia were invited to witness them and to watch the rebuilding of the kingdom. The lesson was well taken, as he intended that it should be. Champa remained a province of Cambodia for the next twenty years, ruled by Jayavarman's nominee. She never recovered from her disastrous defeat, and soon ceased to have any influence in South-east Asia.

Within a very few years, the new capital, Angkor Thom was to be more beautiful than Angkor before the Cham invasion. While his armies were fighting, he concentrated his attentions on a building programme which was to result in the construction of more temples and edifices than in the past twelve reigns. He secured the support of the priests of all sects by masterly intrigue. Although a devout Buddhist, he appointed a Brahman as his chaplain, for the powerful Brahman élite continued to hold sway at Court. He married two princesses who were both ardent Buddhists. The second wife was a Buddhist scholar of international reputation, and for the first decade of his reign he adapted the cult of the god-king to the Buddhist faith. Later he was to reject compromise and follow the teachings of Mahayana Buddhism, but as he became old and his empire grew, he became a megalomaniac, and asserted that he was the reincarnation of Buddha. The stone faces show him in the guise of the Mahayanist Bodhisattva or the Lokesvara. All architecture was Buddhist in style. Throughout his reign, Mahayanist Buddhism was the most widely practised religion in Angkor.

Although the builders went ahead with furious haste, so much so that fearful blunders were made in the rebuilding of the temples, and the construction of others, Jayavarman saw that it would be years before the damage done to Angkor would be repaired. In the meantime, he wanted a temporary city where he could conduct affairs of state and entertain. Accordingly, he built Preah Khan, or the 'Fortunate City of Victory'—again to commemorate the victory over the Chams—but also in memory of his father; and Ta Prohm to the memory and worship of his mother. He also built the lovely Banteai Kdei; an outstanding gem of Khmer architecture called Neak Pean, which he had built on an island; Banteai Chmar and the huge bathing pool, Sra Srang.

He was one of the great social reformers of the Khmers, possibly the only one to achieve any marked success with a programme designed to alleviate distress and treat diseases. His work in this field was staggering in its magnitude and ramifications. He built over 100 hospitals and staffed them with Khmer and foreign doctors. In order to encourage visitors and pilgrims from all over the kingdom and other countries to visit the brilliant capital which was taking shape, he had 150 inns or rest houses constructed on roads which led to Angkor.

The Khmer Empire had never known such an extensive building programme. Looking back over the centuries, it would appear that almost the entire nation was mobilized in a building project which threw up temples, mausoleums, libraries and memorials with such frantic haste that one wonders whether his obsession for seeing the capital one huge construction region was greater than his obsession with death, although he was still reigning and apparently in full possession of his faculties when he was well over 90. It is also possible that he never completely recovered from the shock of seeing his flattened capital and after that only by the construction of more and more buildings, loftier, more massive and sacred than ever, could he efface it from his memory.

His compassion for the suffering and aged contrasted harshly with the callous disregard of his officials for the slaves. They toiled until they dropped dead in the temples they were erecting they were crushed to death by the heavy boulders which were dislodged, overbalanced or fell from the hoists upon their exhausted bodies. They toiled in the quarries, hewing the sandstone for facing and the laterite for hard work and pavings and transporting it long distances from quarry to temple. Angkor Thom was built on the bodies of thousands of slaves; those who survived cursed the temple and the memory of its founder.

Thousands more laboured in the jungle, cutting down the huge trees to provide the wood for the supports, ceilings, doors and engraving. And the orders continued to pour from the royal palace—more stone, more wood and more slaves.

As more temples were completed, so more priests and officials were appointed to run them. A vast revenue was required for their upkeep, and this could only be obtained from the ordinary people. Thousands of villages were allocated to one temple, tens of thousands of officials and hundreds of dancers employed in their service, while an army of labourers, masons, sculptors and artists were engaged on constructional work. The festivals and ceremonies which were held inside the temples, and which were attended only by the privileged élite, must have been time-consuming affairs. An inscription on a stele records that in the course of one festival over 165,000 wax candles were used up. Sexual excesses were practised according to a ritual and were common.

During his reign, the Khmer empire reached its apogee, but his fantastic extravagance was to impoverish the kingdom and lead to its eventual downfall. The hundreds of faces which still stare from the crumbling walls, or peer at one from the vegetation into which they have crashed are faces of Jayavarman VII in the guise of the Buddha; and Buddhism was the dominant religion of his reign. Suryavarman II had blended the worship of Vishnu and Siva in such a way as to substitute a Vishnuraja for a *Devaraja* at Angkor Wat. Jayavarman the megalomaniac substituted a Buddharaja with its centre at the Bayon. In 1933, a French archaeologist unearthed an enormous Buddha image in a pit under the central tower of the Bayon, and it was generally agreed that the Buddhist monks concealed it there during the swing back to Saivism after Jayavarman's death, when the cult of the *linga* replaced that of the Buddha.

He expected that everyone, high-born or low, should be concerned with the future existence in the next world of their god-king, and sternly rebuked and sometimes dismissed any minister, general or ambassador who did not show evidence of sufficient interest. A large number of the temples collapsed only a few years after his reign because of bad and hasty workmanship.

Hundreds of Buddhist monks made their way from India to

Angkor. Many came from the Buddhist centre of Nalanda, which had been invaded and sacked by the Moslems. They lived in the capital and quickly made a tremendous impact upon the people. To offset in advance any criticism which might come from the Brahmans, he was careful to see that the temple mountain, the construction of which was expected of every king, was duly established in a prominent place, but he was satisfied beyond any doubt that Buddhism supplied a scientific and reasonable explanation of the universe. The *linga* was replaced by a statue of Buddha in most temples. There were images of Buddha seated on a coiled *naga* with the fanned out multi-headed hood reared over it in protection. Jayavarman in his role of a living Buddha was assimilated after death with the Buddha, and his salvation ensured.

There is no evidence of any religious strife during his reign. Siva and Vishnu had each passed through periods of popularity and decline. The masses had known Buddhism in the country from time immemorial. Now that the god-king was a Buddhist, it was accepted that the realm would show a close affinity with his faith.

What the court and the ruling classes completely failed to realise was that Buddhism in the Khmer empire was not transitory but was becoming deeply rooted. It was spreading all over the empire, consolidating its strength mainly in the capital.

Angkor Thom became more beautiful and majestic as his reign lengthened. Its construction demonstrated that the king was both a visionary and a realist. It was built in the form of a square, surrounded by an 8-mile wall of laterite, instead of the simple earthworks which had been a feature of the lay-out and defence system of Khmer capitals in previous reigns.

He had retained those buildings which it had been possible to rebuild, and constructed so many more that the old capital—which had stood on the same site—bore little resemblance to the new one. The Bayon was constructed in the centre, south of the ancient palace. It is considered to be the most fantastic of all Khmer architectural edifices, with magnificent bas-reliefs, rich in detail and variety. They cover the entire surface of the walls.

The Khmer sculptors were noted for their sense of humour, and one can imagine one of them saying, "Jayavarman"—for he mixed more freely with his subjects than did any previous king—

"Jayavarman VII, god-king and Buddha, this is your life!" Two hundred massive stone faces, all representations of the god-king, gazed out expressionless into the distance. Historical events, wars, life at court, campaigns, victory parades and such mundane subjects as the ubiquitous camp follower about to pursue the oldest profession of all, a small boy stealing fruit from a sleeping stall-keeper and a cow suckling her calf—there are many others. Gigantic faces stared from the four towers. In the central sanctuary he had an image of Buddha installed and also images of the highest officials in the land in an attitude of worship of the god-king.

Access to the capital city was provided by four axial gates, one for each of the four cardinal points, but a fifth, on the east side, and more stately than the others, led to the royal palace, the residence of the king. The architects did not depart from the long-established traditions of Khmer architecture in the design of these gates. They were intended to be a replica, on a smaller scale, of the temple mountain in the centre of the city, whose magic powers were transmitted to the four cardinal points.

The splendid causeways which crossed the moat gave the city a magnificent approach, and here the architects, sculptors and builders worked under close supervision, for the work was not only arduous but called for a high degree of craftsmanship. For they were lined by long rows of squatting stone giants and demi-gods facing each other, and supporting or tugging at huge stone *nagas* which formed the balustrades, and whose multi-heads and flared hoods reared high up. This was intended to be the most vivid representation of the now familiar Churning of the Sea of Milk, and Jayavarman was well aware that the numerous visitors would stop to admire the *nagas*.

At the entrance to the city a huge inscription proclaimed to all "The City of Yasodharapura [Angkor Thom] was taken to wife by the King for the procreation of the welfare of the Universe".

The *naga* exercised a mystic appeal over the Khmers for centuries. In Jayavarman's time, it was looked upon as a magic bridge or staircase leading to the abode of the gods. The temple was considered to be a flying palace. The simple Khmer believed that in passing between the stone rainbows he arrived at the dwelling of the Lord Buddha.

According to one popular legend, the early Khmers looked upon the *naga* as a deity which glided gracefully through the forests of the Tonlé Sap. It was a creature of great beauty and gorgeous colours. It delighted in lazing by the shores of lakes. One day, a daughter of Indra appeared, and stood for some minutes admiring a flock of white egrets in the water. The deity awoke, stared in admiration at the daughter who was of surpassing loveliness, and fell immediately in love. His heart told him that his long search was ended. He had found his mate. They were married. *Naga* fathered the Khmer race.

Towards the end of his reign, Jayavarman VII tired of military campaigns. He ordered home the large army of occupation he had placed in Champa. It was to prove a fearful blunder, for the defence of the frontier was seriously weakened and the Chams began to give active aid to his enemies. The cynics at court remarked that he needed more temples, and preferred builders to soldiers; therefore he had brought them back to Angkor to train them to dig and build.

Not only temples, but more hospitals were built and these appear to have been adequately staffed and equipped. An inscription found among the ruins of one of them recorded that there were two doctors, each assisted by a man and two women; two storekeepers, whose duty it was to give medicines to the patients; two cooks, who were also responsible for cleaning and fetching fuel and water; two servitors to prepare the offerings to Buddha, fourteen hospital attendants, six women to heat the water and grind the medicines, two women to pound the rice. This put the staff at a total of thirty-six. The list of provisions included honey, sugar, camphor, sesame, spices, black mustard, cumin, nutmeg, coriander, fennel, cardoman, ginger, cinnamon, myrobalan, vinegar etc. At least twelve inscriptions today prove the existence of Jayavarman's hospitals.

He made an effort, although rather belated, to develop the Chinese trade. Embassies had been exchanged, but the frenzied haste and preoccupation with his fantastic building programme lost him much of what could have been a rich source of income. He failed to see that with the increase in maritime trade with China through the Red Sea or the South China Sea, other nations were clamouring for markets.

Peking sent envoys to Angkor to press for more concessions. Their ships sailed right into Angkor with cargoes of mercury, glass, gold, porcelain and sulphur, and took back copper and tin from the Kulen mines, kingfisher feathers, and rhinoceros horns. There is no record of their ships bringing with them ballast in the form of those terrifying giant figures of men which they left behind in so many of the countries with which they traded. Cambodia could take all the imports, and the Chinese captains gladly accepted all the freight that Jayavarman's exporters could give them.

The administration he established was expensive and unwieldy. There was a graded hierarchy of courts, at the top of which was the king as supreme judge. The empire was divided into districts governed by a hierarchy from viceroys to village chiefs. A civil service system consisted of a super-abundance of officials who duplicated each other's work. Express couriers looked after urgent business in the capital. There was a highly privileged Court of Astrologers. Trade between the capital and the provinces, and from one city to another, was organised by a group of officials who also controlled all markets from small to large. This army of officials was costly to maintain, but what was worse, the bribery and corruption created wholesale misery and deep-rooted resentment.

That the kingdom was renowned as the centre of culture, learning and the arts is beyond all doubt, and for this enviable reputation Jayavarman VII was responsible. Scholars from all over the world were attracted to Angkor because of its high civilization. Their own scholars enjoyed a prestige higher than in any previous reign, although they were held in great esteem during the reign of Jayavarman II. A new designation, that of 'King of Professors' was created, and students came to sit at the feet of the great men.

The reign concluded with the emergence of two problems which were to have tremendous impact upon the empire. One was the enormous influence of Buddhism upon the masses. This had increased rapidly all over the entire empire, due largely to the encouragement it had received right from the accession to the throne of the first Buddhist king. It appealed to the people. There were few temples and no elaborate pageantry. Monks and missionaries had arrived in large numbers from India and Siam, and had quickly established friendly relations with the people among whom they lived. The life they followed which was one of austerity, poverty, solitude and meditation contrasted vividly with the luxury and aloofness of the priest-cult. The State religion was undermined, but not deliberately so, by these soft spoken and devoted followers of the Enlightened One.

Another was the danger from a slave population, which was now far greater than ever before and among which were leaders who plotted in the rice fields and who had no difficulty in persuading their hordes of followers to acquire weapons and conceal them in their squalid dwellings of bamboo and atap, ready for the day when the signal would be given.

There was also the problem of opium addiction and drugs concocted from the fermentation of rice and the mixture of other additives. The upper classes used these drugs freely, for they were easily acquired and even the poor could get them. From the death of Jayavarman, opium-taking was to become more widespread, for the poppy flourished. It had always been easy to obtain a supply of opium in South-east Asia. Some archaeologists maintain that architects and sculptors were drug addicts and that the effects of the drug can be seen in the architecture.

Another serious problem he had created was the deforestation of the land. Trees had been cut down in vast numbers and the wood used for building. This uprooting of the 'plugs of the soil' as they are called, caused disastrous floods in the rainy season.

Then Angkor economy and the very existence of the people, particularly the million and more who lived in the capital, depended upon a system of water utilization. King Suryavarman II had perfected an irrigation system which was the wonder of the region. The Chams had destroyed much of it, but in the early years of Jayavarman's reign it had been repaired, improved and extended. In the past twenty-five years, however, it had suffered gross neglect.

Another cause of deep concern to the more far-sighted at court was the warlike conduct of the neighbouring Siamese. They were establishing principalities, and looking out for the rich prizes of conquest. On the opposite border, the Vietnamese were launching foraging raids into Khmer territory. The Mongols were watching these hostile acts with benevolent eyes, and were soon to come out into the open.

Jayavarman was blissfully unaware of the dangers from outside which threatened the magnificent capital, just as he paid scant regard to the menace from within, or else he was convinced that he could meet and overcome them. To his mind, he had given his enormous population a faith and this was demonstrated by the pageant of temples he had built and which would endure long after he had gone to join his god. This faith would sustain them. One is tempted to reflect upon their possible reactions when the roofs and walls of so many of the temples began to crack and crash. Did they regard it as an omen or did they know what the builders knew—that the frenzy of haste, the bad workmanship and the sabotage by some of the more enlightened slaves were responsible?

Be that as it may, Jayavarman in his nineties continued to drive in procession through the Victory Gate to survey the 20-foot stone walls, which were pierced with five triple-towered gateways each one crowned with four stone faces which appeared to watch for any threat to the capital.

His death came in A.D. 1218 and marked the end of an era.

Here it is both timely and helpful to trace the evolution of the institution of the cult of the god-king from the days of the early Khmer kings to the one who believed himself to be so far above his fellow humans, the greatest of all god-kings, Jayavarman VII, the living Buddha.

The worship of the god-king is a subject which has intrigued and astonished all students of Khmer history. In his interesting article in *La Revue Française*, Bernard P. Groslier wrote:

> The kings of Angkor were too often concerned with personal glory and undertook too many wars. But above all, with the support of a brilliant and powerful court which upheld their desire for power, these kings gradually lost all contact with their subjects. The Khmer *élite*, influenced by the highest Indian culture, played an essential part in the growth of the empire . . . very soon, the Khmer kings were completely obsessed by life after death—the beyond. Not content with being worshipped in life, they were determined, before death to assure for themselves a perpetual cult in their memory, and to be convinced that they would be remembered by identifying themselves with a divinity. The temple-mountain where the king celebrated the universal ritual during his lifetime became a funerary temple after his death. . . .

Bernard P. Groslier maintains that this is to some extent an explanation of the numerous monuments at Angkor, and he goes on to say that in the case of Jayavarman VII, this fear of death was such a consuming obsession that the country was "littered with sanctuaries hurriedly put up to charm away this annihilation which he feared all the time was near".

George Coedès gives an interesting viewpoint in his *Pour Mieux Comprendre Angkor*. He says: "The pre-Angkorian era and during the first part of the Angkorian period until the end of the tenth century, shows that the gods were given the same title as the king, the princes and the high dignitaries. This was *Kamrateng anh* which meant 'Master'. From the second half of the tenth century onwards, the term *Kamrateng jagat* replaced *Kamrateng anh*. It signified 'Master of the Universe' to designate the gods. It possessed the advantage of creating a clear distinction between the god's world and that of men."

The royal *linga* in which the essence of royalty lay was set up in the pyramid or temple mountain erected in the centre of the capital and became the centre of the visible and cosmic world. It was the symbol of absolute monarchy.

It was accepted that the kings in turn were in communion with Siva or Vishnu through the intermediary of the Brahman priest who deliberately conveyed the impression that the god was the royal god. In the tenth century Jayavarman IV succeeded in transforming the royal god into a national god. This god was inscribed on some pyramids as "*Kamrateng jagat ta pajya*" or "The Master of the universe which is the king".

And so the kings were deified. *Devaraja* was to take on a new meaning, a greater significance, a much more powerful status. The kings were to be proclaimed as the living Siva or Vishnu. *Devaraja* taught the masses that the king came from above, with supreme, divine powers.

George Coedès sums up the position relative to the gods and the kings in his impressions of Angkor Wat. "The Vishnu which worshipped there was not the old Hindu god, but the King Suryavarman II, identified with Vishnu after his death, dwelling in his tomb, decorated with *apsaras*, like Vishnu in his celestial palace."

Although thousand of his subjects toiled over the years to build the fabulous Angkor Wat and later, other temples, the temple was therefore not intended as a place of worship for them but rather for the king's special pleasures and use in life. However, the people were admitted on special fête days, and they came to prostrate themselves but not so much to the god, be it Siva, Vishnu or Buddha. They worshipped the image of the god-king.

Jayavarman VII ordered that all refer to him as Jayavarmadeva, which name ended in the suffix *deva* or god. The kings who succeeded him never achieved his 'immortality' status among the masses. He was unique. After the fall of Angkor, the Khmer kings gradually lost their proud and awe-inspiring titles, although the divine authority which the still powerful Brahman priest élite maintained was passed down to them was accepted by the masses, although less blindly and without the same demonstrations of adoration and adulation. Angkor had crashed and with it the image of the god-king which had dominated every aspect of Khmer life for centuries.

The Khmer kings became known as *Dharmaraja* or 'issue of the old established order' and *rajadhirajaramadhipati* or 'great master, king of kings'. Then this too, declined, and the chaos which continued intermittently for centuries gave Cambodia either kings without power, or no kings at all. The memory of the god-kings faded, and with them the history of those who tried to rule the disintegrated kingdom.

FIVE

The Imperial Envoy from Peking

The emperor Timur who succeeded Kublai Khan, sent an embassy to Angkor in 1296 to make a detailed report on conditions in the Khmer kingdom. A member of the small party was Chou Ta-kuan, who spent over a year in the country; and his report languished for centuries in the imperial archives.

In 1902, a French translation by the celebrated sinologist Paul Pelliot was published in the *Bulletin de l'École Française d'Extrême Orient*. The author has translated and adapted his own version from the French.

Chou Tak-kuan was obviously a shrewd observer of the customs and activities of the Khmers. He travelled widely and mixed with all classes of people. His report was comprehensive and illuminating, and its accuracy was proved some 600 years later by the experiences of the team of experts appointed by the French government to reconstitute and reconstruct the ruins. They found that this description of "54 gigantic and terrible genii" facing each other across the causeway corresponded to the number they had discovered. More evidence of the truth of the account of this eye-witness was provided by his reference to the gold Sword of State, the description of the parasols borne above the heads of princes and ministers, and other statements which the French archaeologists and naturalists themselves had made when they had sweltered and toiled in the Cambodian jungle some years before the report had come to light. Now they had more to go on.

Chou Ta-kuan gives us a fascinating picture of life in the great capital. We are told of its customs, some of which are rather harrowing, such as the rites practised in the deflowering of young girls, the forcible removal of human gall, and the punishments. It is a factual account of the position of slaves, of justice, horses, agriculture, royal processions, immigrants, food, wine, religion, animal and bird life, etc.

Another Angkor Wat bas-relief. The goddess is supported by sacred
geese and thus represents a floating palace

Angkor Wat: bas-relief showing the descent into hell

His description dealing with the walled city is vivid and detailed. He says:

there are five huge re-inforced gates. Beyond the wall there is a very wide moat, access to which is provided by five causeways. On each side of the bridge are fifty-four stone gods who are gigantic and frightening. The parapets of the bridge are built entirely of stone, constructed in the form of two enormous serpents, each with nine heads which the giants support with their hands, and give the impression that they are trying to prevent from escaping. Above each gate there are five stone Buddhas, their faces turned towards the four cardinal points. The middle head is gilded. Elephants in stone have been sculptured on both sides of the doors. The ramparts are built of huge blocks of stone placed one on top of the other. Trees have been planted at intervals along the ramparts. Inside the wall are more gates. These are closed at night, and sentries are always on guard. Dogs, and criminals who have had their toes cut off are not allowed inside the gates. A golden tower marks the centre of the kingdom. It is flanked by more than twenty stone towers and many hundreds of stone houses. A bridge of gold stretches from the East gate; two golden lions have been erected left and right of the bridge, and eight golden Buddhas stand below the stone galleries.

About a furlong to the north, there is a bronze tower which is higher than the golden one, and from the top the view is most impressive. At the foot of the tower there are more stone galleries. Another furlong to the north, one comes across the royal residence. In the private apartments there is another golden tower. I think that it is these edifices which have given the country the title "Rich and noble Cambodia" by foreign visitors. The eastern lake is about a mile and a quarter from the walled town. In the middle, there is a stone tower in which reclines a stone Buddha with water flowing continuously from his navel.

On the banks many stone houses have been built. The North gate has a square tower of gold, a lion and a Buddha in gold, and an elephant, bull, and horse, all in bronze.

His description of the royal palace* sheds some light on the authority of the cult of the god-king, class distinction and the belief of the natives in old legends. It is possible that he realised that these beliefs were deliberately fostered in order to present the king, who was so far above them all, as a supreme being to be

* Only temples were built of stone. Royal palaces were built of wood although richly carved, with exquisite flooring and with fine furnishings.

worshipped. The royal palace, government buildings and houses of the ruling class faced east. The palace itself was situated to the north of the golden tower and bridge. These buildings were made of yellow porcelain. The roof of the royal palace was made up of yellow glazed tiles which Chou Ta-kuan at first thought were gold. The private apartments of the nobles were tiled with lead. Only the higher classes were permitted to have tiled roofs, and the degree of nobility was decided by the size and grandeur of the residence. The poor had to be content with thatched roofs.

In the royal palace, there were spacious verandas and roofed corridors. His description is quite lyrical, and he comments rather wistfully that so much that was beautiful was hidden from the ordinary visitor: "I have heard that in the interior of the palace there are many marvellous places, but the palace was well guarded and it was impossible for me to see them for myself." However, he wrote of royal audiences held at the palace where the king sat on a terrace before a gilded window with some forty or fifty mirrors on pillars. When the hour for the king's arrival approached, music was heard, and immediately men began to blow on conch shells. Two ladies of the royal household crawled to the gold-framed window, and drew aside the curtains to reveal the king seated with the sacred sword in his hands. In this position they were required to remain until the conch shells were silent. They were then permitted to sit back and face the king.

The royal sleeping quarters were situated at the top of the tower. A spirit in the form of a serpent with nine heads, who was master of the realm, changed his form to that of a girl and appeared every night before the king. He was required to have intercourse with her, after which he was free to go to his wives or concubines. "If the spirit was absent one evening, the king would die, but if he absented himself, disaster would overtake the kingdom. He had one wife who lived in quarters adjoining his own apartment, and four principal wives for each cardinal point of the compass. In addition, there were numerous concubines and dancing girls."

In connection with these legends, it should be remembered that a large number of the Khmers worshipped the spirits or gods of rivers, woods and fields. In Cambodia today, there are still a large number of animists as well as a general acceptance of a spirit world.

Chou Ta-kuan tells us that there were some 5,000 girls in the palace. It was customary for parents of beautiful daughters to present them to the king.

One realizes the extent to which the god-king was worshipped by reading Chou Ta-kuan's description of a ceremonial drive through the capital. Such an occasion, and they were frequent, was a glittering and colourful pageant.

Cavalry led the procession, followed by hundreds of standards and pennants. Massed bands came next and were interspersed at intervals along the long line of route. Behind the bands, large numbers of dancing girls glided by. Each one wore flowers in her hair and carried tall, lighted candles in her hands. After them walked the palace maidens. They passed by in their hundreds, carrying gold and silver vessels, trays of precious stones, ornaments, including ropes of pearls. Right behind them marched the exclusive King's Bodyguard. This was a female preserve and was composed of tall and good looking Amazons. They carried shields and lances.

A delightful sight was provided by a cavalcade of goat carriages and horse-chariots, decorated with precious metals which sparkled brilliantly in the sunshine. The numerous nobility followed. Among them were the large numbers of princes, ministers and courtiers. This was a colourful spectacle, for they were mounted on elephants which were decorated with gold rings on their tusks, the number corresponding to the rank of the rider, who sat under a red parasol which protected him from the sun.

The king's wives and concubines had assembled behind the nobles and they were conveyed in varied forms of transport. A large number reclined in palanquins which were richly decorated, others rode in howdahs, some in chariots, while others walked. They had all taken pains to appear at their best, and the result was enchanting.

There was much excitement among the spectators as the procession of wives and concubines drew to an end, for they knew that it heralded the appearance of the king. He rode on an elephant with gilded tusks, standing erect under a red and gold canopy. He was adorned with jewels. There was a golden diadem on his head, a chain of pearls around his neck, gold bracelets set with cat's eyes on his wrists and ankles, and many rings on his fingers. In his hands he held the sacred Sword of State, the symbol of divine majesty.

In the museum of Phnom Penh I was shown a sword which, up to the fall of the monarchy in 1970, was used in connection with coronation ceremonies, and I was assured by the guide that it was the same sword which was used all those centuries ago.

The spectators were forbidden to gaze upon the face of the king. The law required that they prostrated themselves, keeping their heads to the ground until he had passed, but one can assume that many ventured to take a surreptitious peep. The royal escort consisted of a detachment of cavalry and foot soldiers carrying long white parasols.

Despite the beliefs in the king's divinity, the god-king himself took precautions for his own personal safety, however much he may have been assured of his omnipotence, immortality and the vigilance of his personal escort. Chou Ta-kuan writes that "he wears such effective armour that no knife or arrow could penetrate it". He had watched him ride in special processions on several occasions during the year he spent in Angkor, and he observed the well-armed bodyguard.

The palace itself, included a small city of women and young girls. What tremendous power the favourites wielded! And woe betide any man who offended them! Chou Ta-kuan tells of a room in the royal palace where, on a raised dais, the jewelled beds glittered, and of a palanquin of gold, whose loveliness was enhanced by banners and shafts with gold handles, and of the priceless jewels which adorned the favourites. "When the king left the palace, his chair was borne on the shoulders of the amazons of the court." Truly a matriarchal establishment! However, we must not be hard on these Khmer kings who ruled 700 years ago, for when the French government established its protectorate over Cambodia in 1863, it was found that the reigning king employed 800 women in the palace, and that many were of outstanding beauty!

Once the king's procession had made its complete tour, he was conducted back to the private apartments of the palace, where the girls danced before him with fans and banners, dressed in cloth of gold and jewels, with flowers in their hair and waving lotus buds.

Another vivid picture of the god-king is painted on the occasion of a ceremonial visit to one of the temples of Siva. We are told that he was seated on an elephant, dressed as a Khmer god, with a crown encrusted with pearls on his head, and a jewelled girdle around his waist. The elephant was an impressive sight with glittering head-piece and harness, scarlet and gold bands around the trunk and legs. Large numbers of youths and girls carried banners and acclaimed the king, singing his virtues. The escort was composed of the commander-in-chief of the Royal Regiment of Elephants, the Regiment of Lancers and fleet captains. In this manner, the god-king passed through streets lined with his prostrate subjects, while the secret police kept a sharp look-out for anyone whose attitude was not as cringing as they judged it should be.

Chou Ta-kuan has much to say about the judiciary system. The death sentence was formerly carried out by decapitation or strangling, but this had been replaced by digging a trench and burying the criminals alive. Lesser punishments inflicted were the amputation of fingers, legs or hands. The nose was sometimes cut off. There was no law against adultery, and the courts appear to have turned a blind eye to direct action by the husband or offended party provided that the punishment was not too severe, and did not cause a public disturbance. For example, if a husband caught the adulterer in the act, he squeezed his legs between two blocks. The pain was soon unbearable but was continued until freedom was obtained by the handing over of all his possessions. Flogging was a fairly common punishment for minor offences.

A thief was generally punished by imprisonment and being put to the question. Trial by ordeal was normal procedure. A suspect was required to plunge his hands in boiling oil, and was judged innocent if they were unscathed when taken out. Chou Ta-kuan was not impressed by this method and describes it as "one of the strange customs of the barbarians".

Inquests were unknown. If a man found a corpse outside his house, he attached cords to it and dragged it to some desolate place where he left it for the wild animals and birds to devour. This expediency avoided much inconvenient questioning. If two men claimed ownership of the same article, or one alleged injury by the other, and it could not be established as to who was the guilty partner, they would each be placed in one of the twelve stone towers outside the royal palace. There they remained for several days, watched by their accusers and supporters.

Apparently nothing was done to them during their period of incarceration. They were fed by their friends, and no doubt given moral support. It is not known whether they were exhorted to confess, or to persist in maintaining their innocence. No physical punishment appears to have been administered, nor was the threat of it used as an inducement by the authorities. After a prescribed period, both were released from the tower and allowed to go about their ordinary business. It was generally accepted that punishment would take its course, "for the one who was guilty will have contracted some illness, such as ulcers, catarrh or malignant fever. The other one will have been free of disease." This is, according to Chou Ta-kuan, 'Heavenly Justice' and illustrates the supernatural powers of the god of this country.

There were a number of ceremonies and exhibitions of a lavish nature which made life very exciting and colourful at times, and which the poor could see. The advent of the New Year, Chou Ta-kuan was surprised to find, was celebrated in November instead of February or March, as in China. Then followed the commencement of the seasons; wrestling bouts; the Throwing the Ball, the Grand Procession, in which the entire population of the capital moved past the royal palace; the Washing of the Images of the Buddha, when all the images were assembled before the palace and washed in the presence of the king. Half-way through the year, there was the spectacle of 'sailing ships over land'. The king stood in a summer house where he was able to take part in the fête. The following month, they enjoyed the ceremony of Burning the Rice, which was very popular with women, who travelled from over a wide area by elephant or carriage to take part. The rice crop had ripened, and the festival was held outside the south door as an offering to the Buddha.

Dancing to Music, another special event, took place during the eighth month. Actors and musicians came to the royal palace to take part. Fights between boars and elephants were arranged. To these ceremonies and functions, the king invited ambassadors from foreign courts.

Chou Ta-kuan appears to have enjoyed the celebrations which ushered in the New Year. A large platform providing a seating capacity for more than 1,000 persons was erected in front of the royal palace, and decorated with lanterns and flowers. Every night for the next two weeks, scaffolding and high masts were erected opposite the platform and four or five pyramids constructed, to the apices of which rockets and crackers were attached. When night came the king presided over the fireworks display, when flying rockets were sent up very high. Crackers as large as cannons made a terrific noise and shook the city with the force of the explosion.

Chou Ta-kuan has much to say on the subject of diseases, including leprosy, but the causes he puts forward for the illnesses which afflict the people are difficult to accept. Too frequent baths and washing of the head are, in his opinion, the main reasons. There were many lepers about, but no one objected to eating and sleeping with them. There was even a Leper King, but he was not shunned because he had contracted this terrible disease. He concludes this paragraph with a weighty pronouncement, and one can imagine him writing it after careful consideration and due solemnity. "In my humble opinion, one contracts this disease if sexual excesses are followed immediately by over indulgence in baths."

Chou Ta-kuan describes the government ministers and the excessive pomp which surrounds the offices they hold, and comments, rather cynically, that "in addition to ministers, generals and astronomers and other officials, there is a whole horde of minor state employees, just as we have". Apparently princes occupied the highest posts, and it was customary for them to offer their daughters to the king as royal concubines. When the officials travelled, they were provided with an escort, the size and dignity of which corresponded to their rank. The most important rode in palanquins with golden shafts and four parasols with golden handles. Then came escorts of palanquins with golden shafts, and one parasol with a golden handle, to the most junior who were provided with only one parasol with a silver handle. However, even officials in this category wielded considerable power. Administration was clearly overloaded with officials, and the cost to the country was enormous. Chou Ta-kuan did not fail to notice that the parasols were made of red taffeta from China. The fringes reached to the ground. The plainer umbrellas were made from green oiled silk with short fringes.

His description of the ceremony of deflowering young girls is rather harrowing. Those of rich families were deflowered between the ages of 7 and 9 by Buddhist or Taoist priests employed by their parents, but girls of poor families had to wait until they were eleven. Every year, the authorities chose a day in the month which co-incided with the fourth Chinese moon, and publicised it throughout the country. Families with daughters of the appropriate age notified the local official, who sent them a candle on which a mark had been made. On the actual day, the candle was lighted at nightfall, and when it had burnt down to the mark, the time for *tchen-t'an* or deflowering had arrived. Up to a month before this date, the parents had selected a Buddhist or Taoist priest. In actual practice, certain priests had a regular clientèle and were booked in advance by rich families, but those in poor circumstances had little choice, although here it was usual for a priest to perform the act free as a charitable deed.

Those priests reserved by the rich families received generous payment in wine, rice, silk, linen and silver objects which could be worth 200 or 300 ounces of Chinese silver. A priest was permitted to deflower only one girl and had to reject all other advances once he had been chosen. On the night of *tchen-t'an*, the parents prepared a lavish banquet if their circumstances allowed, but all did their best to lay on some kind of entertainment and provide refreshment. When all was ready, the parents called for the priest, the rich ones setting out in palanquins and bands. Two pavilions of silk of different colours were constructed. The girl sat in one, the priest in another. It was impossible to hear what was said as the noise from the bands was deafening. At the agreed time, the priest entered the girl's pavilion and deflowered her by hand.

Chou Ta-kuan here includes some unpleasant details in his report, and then goes on to tell us that there was many who maintained that the priest had actual intercourse with the girl, but as Chinese visitors were not permitted to witness events of this nature, "I cannot say exactly what takes place." However, at daybreak, the priest was escorted home with the usual palanquins, bands and banners. The girl then had to be purchased back from him with gifts of materials, or else she would remain his property and would not be free to marry. Chou Ta-kuan was most specific as to detail when recording this particular custom for he concludes with the statement "this particular ceremony took place on the sixth night of the fourth moon of the year *ting-yeou* of the period *ta-to*" (28th April 1297).

Right up to *tchen-t'an*, father mother and daughter slept in the same room; henceforth the girl was excluded from the parental apartment, and was free to come and go as she pleased without supervision or restraint.

He appears to be shocked by what he regarded as the loose morals of the women. In his report on confinements, he tells of a young girl who had a baby and took it with her to the baths the following day. The women were very lascivious. One or two days after the confinement they desired sexual relations with their husbands, and if he did not respond they left him. If the husband was called away on business, all was well for a few nights, but after about ten days they would argue, "I am not a spirit, how can I sleep alone?" They aged quickly, due to their many confinements, and at the age of 20 or 30 they resembled Chinese women of 40 or 50. Angkor, too, had its prostitutes. Every day, he says, groups of ten or more women loiter in the main square. Their chief target was the Chinese for they were generous. "It is hideous and shocking!"

However, it was not their immoral lives which was the sole cause of their premature aging. They worked very hard. The women of the upper classes he considered to be captivating. Their skins were as white as jade, for they were never exposed to the sun. This contrasted violently with the black skins and coarse features of the vast majority of the population. The women were the shopkeepers. Their shops consisted of items placed around a mat on which the woman sat. She was required to pay rent to a mandarin for her shop. The Chinese visitors had to be on their guard for the shopkeepers were out to swindle them. He was disgusted by some of the habits of the women. "Some urinate standing. It is ridiculous!" he wrote.

His constant references to his hosts as barbarians are not without their light side. He is convinced of the superiority of China in all things and leaves the emperor in no doubt as to his views.

Clothing did not present a big problem. Everyone from the king down wore a chignon, and all went about with bare shoulders. Even the higher classes were content to wear a length of material as a loin cloth, but when they went out into the streets, they wrapped a larger piece over the smaller one. A large quantity of the cloth was made in Siam and Champa, but best quality came from India, and was in great demand on account of its fine thread and texture. Women were allowed to paint the soles of their feet and the palms of their hands red, but, with the exception of the king, this privilege was not extended to the men. Both sexes used perfume made from sandalwood, musk and other essences, and the women never missed an opportunity to display their breasts.

He was an interested although sometimes puzzled observer of the three religions, the ritual and the priests. He is not sure of the functions of the *pan-k'i* and their ritual and printed dogma. It is most likely that these were the court Brahmans, a very exclusive sect, mainly concerned with the ceremonies of the palace, the safety of the Sword of State, and other royal regalia. They wore a cord of white thread around their necks, and it was never removed.

The *tch'ou-kou* were Buddhist monks or *bonzes*. He says that they shaved their heads, wore a saffron robe which left the right shoulder bare, and went about bare-foot. Their temple roofs were tiled, and the interiors contained only one image, which was of the Buddha. They ate fish and meat but did not drink wine. They had only one meal a day which they took with the family which had invited them. Eating out must have been customary, for there were no kitchens in the Buddhist temples. Some of the senior Buddhist monks were allowed to ride in a palanquin with shafts, under a parasol with gold or silver handle. They were consulted by the king on affairs of state. There were no Buddhist nuns.

The *pa-sseu-wei* were Brahman priests. They dressed like ordinary people, except for a piece of red or white material which they wore around their heads. They were not so influential as the Buddhist monks, and their temples were smaller, but they were allowed to tile them. They did not eat in public. Unlike the Buddhists, they had nunneries.

Chou Ta-kuan has much to say about the huge slave population and it is obvious that it made a profound impression on him. "They were acquired with amazing ease. Some people had more than a hundred, middle class families possessed from ten to twenty, and only the poorest of the poor had none at all. The young and strong could be purchased for a hundred pieces of cloth, the old for thirty to forty."

A large number were aborigines rounded up in the mountainous regions. They were of two kinds; those who understood the language, and those who had no language other than their own, and had never lived in a house. A characteristic of this class is that they were to be found wandering continually in the mountains, carrying clay pots on their heads to which they attached great value. They killed wild animals with bows and spears, made a fire to cook them by rubbing sticks together, and after the meal continued on their wanderings. The former class were sold in the towns.

All were subjected to strict discipline. They were not allowed to go out of the house, and inside it they could sit or lie down only under the stairs. If their duties took them upstairs, they were required to salaam and prostrate themselves before commencing their tasks. They addressed their master and mistress as 'father' and 'mother'. If they committed an offence, they were thrashed and had to remain motionless while punishment was inflicted. It was customary to ignore them except for cases of what was considered unsatisfactory work or bad behaviour. They were looked upon as animals, and were bought and sold cheaply. Those who attempted to escape were marked with a blue sign on their foreheads or had iron fetters fixed to their legs or around their necks. It was obvious that Khmer society was based on slave labour.

Chou Ta-kuan's opinion was that they were dangerous and had homicidal tendencies, which perhaps is not surprising. There was certainly an element of prophecy about this judgment. They were definitely a race apart. As the capital was swarming with them, savage treatment was no doubt an expediency to ensure that they did not rebel. This method was to fail in later years. They were known contemptuously as *tchong*, which is one of the biggest insults a free Khmer can level against another. Although male and female slaves copulated freely, the master of the house did not assert his rights. Intercourse with a slave was considered to be degrading, and in any case there were plenty of concubines to satisfy his desires. If a visitor, particularly a Chinese, had relations with one of the girls, the master of the house would refuse to sit with him. Celibacy, or protracted absence from home was no excuse. The guest had not only disgraced himself but brought disgrace on the house. No action was taken when female slaves became pregnant, as they had no civil rights; moreover the slave population was automatically increased by illegitimacy.

Chou Ta-kuan describes the interiors of the houses of the upper classes, and the cooking utensils used by all. Again, he was impressed by the sharp division rank imposed on them all. The middle and lower classes would not dare to be pretentious. They had no furniture, not even a table. Their cooking utensils were of the simplest. They consisted of an earthenware pot in which to cook rice, and an earth stove on which to prepare sauce. Three stones sunk in the ground served as a stove, and coconuts were used as ladles and spoons. Rice was served on Chinese plates of earthenware or copper, and tiny cups fashioned out of leaves were used to help one to sauce. Smaller leaves were employed as spoons and then thrown away. The same procedure was followed when making sacrifices to the gods or Buddha. Wine was drunk from goblets made of pewter, but the poor made do with earthenware vessels.

The nobles and those of the wealthy classes had silver or gold utensils, and for royal festivals they used gold plates of special design. Mats, imported from China were placed on the floor, as well as skins of tigers, panthers and deer. All slept on bamboo matting, although low beds made by the Chinese were just becoming popular.

Official records were written on deerskin or buckskin, with a stick dipped in a powder like Chinese chalk. They wrote in black, from left to right. There were public booths where professional writers would draw up petitions.

It was not the custom for the Khmers to make use of coffins for burials. The disposal of the corpse was done in a manner which contrasted with the pomp and ceremony of the funeral procession. The body was wrapped up in mats and covered with a cloth. Flags, banners and bands accompanied the mourners. Two plates of grilled rice were thrown as the procession continued on its way. The corpse was conveyed outside the city and abandoned in some desolate spot where dogs, vultures and other animals devoured it.

There was a wide variety of imports which included pewter, lacquer trays, mercury, blue porcelain, parchment, saltpetre, sandalwood, musk, canvas, cloth, parasols, iron pots, oils, wooden combs, needles etc.

Chou Ta-kaun states that the most valuable products were kingfisher's feathers, elephant's tusks, rhinoceros horns and beeswax.

Kingfisher's feathers* were much sought after on account of

---

* Sir Osbert Sitwell states in his book *Escape With Me* that the export of kingfisher's feather to China played an important part in the economy of the Khmers, and that the ponds were especially constructed to ensnare the birds. Chou Ta-kuan's account above would indicate that it was difficult to obtain a large quantity. That they were exported to China is beyond doubt, but whether they made any big impact upon the economy is questionable.

their bright and varied colours. However, it was not easy to trap the birds in large numbers as Chou Ta-kuan tells us. He says, "In the dense forests there are ponds which are full of fish. The king-fisher flies over them in search of his prey. The trapper hides in the foliage with a cage in which he has placed a female kingfisher to attract the male. He catches it with a net which he holds in his hand. On some days he catches three or five; sometimes the whole day passes without the unfortunate trapper catching a single bird."

The observant envoy from China reported that among the many birds of the Khmer Empire, the peacock, kingfisher and parrot are not known in China, but vultures, crows, sparrows, storks, cranes, cormorants, wild ducks flew over Angkor in abun-dance. Nor did China have the rhinoceros, the elephant, the wild buffalo which roamed the Khmer forests. Indeed, ancient Cam-bodia was teeming with animal life. There were tigers, panthers, bears, wild boar, monkeys and foxes.

The country was rich in brightly coloured shrubs, flowers and rare trees. Both aquatic flowers and others were more numerous than those in China, and were scented and beautiful. There was a large variety of vegetables: onions, leeks, egg-plants, water-melons, pumpkins, cucumbers and many others which he could not identify. Cotton trees grew higher than the houses.

In the Great Lake there was a never ending supply of fish, the most abundant being carp. All species of fish were found in the sea. There were enormous tortoises and alligators. Giant crocodiles —he says that they were as large as canoes—lazed in the swamps and marshlands.

The Khmers had developed a taste for wine. There were four kinds, honey wine which was prepared by mixing honey and water in equal parts and adding a fermenting compound. *P'ong-ya-sseu*, so named by the natives, for it was the leaf of a special tree, was distilled to produce another wine. Rice, as today, provided the basis of a potent drink. It was called *pao-leng-kio*, which means rice-wine, and was prepared from either cooked or coarse rice. The fourth was obtained from sugar.

There were no restrictions on the preparation of salt, such as existed in other countries of South-east Asia. It was produced by the trapping and subsequent evaporation of sea water.

He does not have a high opinion of the Khmer women's skill in weaving, nor in the use of the needle and in sewing and darning.

"They use bamboo shuttles, fold one end of the cloth around the waist and work on the other. The Siamese immigrants who have settled in the country are far more proficient, and work in silk."

He found that in ship-building, the Khmer methods were slow because they did not use saws. For large ships, they prepared planks with chisels, from branches cut from hard trees with an axe, as in the construction of houses. Iron nails were used, and the ships were covered with non porous leaves secured by laths. Smaller ships were made by hollowing out the trunk and burning it out to the required depth. There were no sails, and the ships were propelled by oars.

There were more than ninety-six provinces, each one under the control of mandarins, and each one fortified with wooden barricades. Even the smallest village had a tower or a temple, and if the size of the population merited the distinction of an official of the high rank of mandarin, one was appointed. On the main roads there was a network of inns where the traveller could rest.

Already cracks in the great Khmer Empire have been recorded as far back as A.D. 1296. The Khmers, who throughout their history had carried war into other countries had recently suffered at the hands of the warring Siamese. He says that villages have been completely devastated.

He writes of a gruesome custom. This was the collection of a jar of human gall in accordance with a demand made by the King of Champa. and it was done annually. During the eighth moon, those appointed to carry out this horrible task were posted at night in well-populated localities. Woe betide the unfortunate wretch who ventured forth at night! He was seized, his head covered with a hood tied by a cord, and his gall removed from the right side by means of a small knife. Chinese citizens could walk about in safety. This was not through fear of the anger of the Peking court. Chou Ta-kuan advances the astonishing explanation that one year the gall of a Chinese had been placed in the jar with the others, causing the contents to rot! He does not enlighten us as to whether it was the Chinese or the barbarians' gall which was the more powerful!

He finds the weather terribly hot and "one is obliged to bathe several times a day, even at night". There were no bath houses, basins or pails. However, every family had a pond, or else two or three families shared one. Men and women went into the pond naked, but children did not bathe with their parents. Even those of good family bathed in this way without shame. The Khmers were obviously a very clean race and they enjoyed taking their baths, although, as stated earlier, Chou Ta-kuan thought that they over-indulged to the detriment of their health.

Evidence of the warlike characteristics of the Khmers is provided by his report on visits to the royal arsenal and barracks. They fought their wars with sabres, daggers, spears linked by a chain and wielded by two pikemen; war machines had been copied from those used in his homeland and included catapults, double crossbows and ballistas mounted on wheels or on the backs of elephants. The hundreds of canoes were fitted with arrow-resisting armour.

His considered opinion that the ruling classes were united in their love of war, luxury and pageantry was undoubtedly correct as was also his summing up of the religious question. He found the entire nation deeply religious. He was surprised by the complete freedom and tolerance of other religions. Siva, Vishnu and Buddha were all represented in the same temple. However, this shrewd observer had noted one vital factor which was to undermine to the point of disintegration the image of the god-king, although this was not the avowed policy of those whose teachings were to destroy it and with it the empire, for the two could not exist without the identification and unity of one with the other. This factual statement, presented simply—for Chou Ta-kuan was never to realise its tremendous significance—was that there were "thousands of Buddhists monks in the streets with their begging bowls."

Buddhism was presenting a united front. Vishnu and Siva had known alternating periods of supremacy, and were now declining in influence.

The "thousands of monks" were preaching the Hinayanist creed of Buddhism, which since the death of Jayavarman VII had gained enormous popularity and was now sweeping the kingdom. This king was, of course, a Buddhist, but, like earlier Buddhist kings of Angkor, he belonged to the Mahayana School. The difference is considerable. The teachings of Hinayana followed on the life and lessons of the Buddha. It taught that man can obtain relief from suffering by following his example. It exercised a tremendous appeal to the humble citizen. Mahayana held that salvation was restricted to a few. It was rich in symbolism, ceremonial and ritual, a much more sophisticated form of Buddhism, with hierarchies of Buddhas. Bodhisattvas and minor gods. At that time, both forms were affected by the creed of the trinity, but now Hinayana was outstripping it as well as the Mahayana. The Siamese were Hinayanists.

Bernard Groslier in his *Angkor Art and Civilization* states that Cambodia owed her existence as a nation to India, in the same way that France was borne from the Roman occupation. It is equally true that India also gave her Buddhism, and this was to play a great part in the dissolution of the Khmer empire.

In spite of the air of detachment in which it appears to have been written, his statement that "in the recent war with the Siamese, the entire Khmer population had to take part" was of tremendous significance. Perhaps he knew that the sun was setting on the mighty Khmer empire.

Chou Ta-kuan made no reference to one remarkable fact. Perhaps he was unaware of it, or else he considered that the history of the Khmers was outside the scope of his report to his emperor. Yet its importance could not be exaggerated. It was that this nation of temple builders had not erected a magnificent new temple since the death of the Mahayanist Buddhist king Jayavarman VII eighty years ago. This left the field wide open to the Hinayanist monks of the saffron robe, who poured into the kingdom to receive a warm welcome, and in time to take it over.

The report ends on a light note. It is perhaps an implied recommendation—one could say a touch of the guide book—in the concluding paragraph. "Rice is plentiful, women easy to find, the houses easy to manage, property easy to manage and business good."

The worthy Chinese envoy could never have imagined that his report would achieve immortality and reveal to the world some of the secrets of the Lost Capital.

(*above*) Gateway to the temple of Preah Viharn. (*below*) The
elephant terrace of Angkor Thom

A tree grows on the summit of a tower of Angkor Thom

SIX

Four Gods Look Down

His successor was Indravarman II who was content to bask in the reflected glory of his dynamic father. He achieved little, but at least he did not build. Nor did Jayavarman VIII, who followed him, and the economy picked up a little. However, this king, who was a grandson of the illustrious emperor of the same name, and who was to reign longer than any other Khmer king, was not satisfied with the reduced prestige of the god-king. For this, he held Buddhism responsible and he soon took steps to curb its influence. He re-established the cult of Brahma, but the godlike image he was determined to reimpose upon the people had faded.

The grim truth was that the great empire was slowly dying, although it was to be a very slow death.

Khmer civilization, indeed the very existence of the Khmer people, depended upon an efficient irrigation system which gave abundant rice yields. These magnificent waterworks had been allowed to deteriorate still further in the 30 years which had passed since Jayavarman VII's death. The canals became clogged, making navigation to the capital increasingly difficult. Plague after plague struck the provinces, interspersed and often accompanied by epidemics of malaria caused by the mosquitoes which bred profusely in the now stagnant swamps. The simple peasant looked at the once magnificent barays and other water reservoirs which his forefathers had died in building, heard in silence the promises of the king's tax collectors that they would be made good, then quietly and secretly folded his tent and stole away. Those that were left realised that they could not thrust back the jungle which invaded the rice paddies. Nor could they continue to make the crushing sacrifices required for the costly life in the temples. Whole villages were abandoned as the headman led his people to places where the rain poured down from the skies in torrents, flooded the land but provided more than enough for their needs.

Yet the dizzy pageant of entertainment continued as before in the capital. The tax collectors contrived to keep the granaries full, and if yields from some provinces were late or fell off, little was done about it.

Jayavarman VIII increased the size of his army to make Angkor Thom safe from attack. The largest force in Khmer history was concentrated within its walls. Temple worship, the processions of the priests, the sacred procession of the king, his identification with the gods, all this continued as before, but he was dissatisfied with the results of his own efforts and those of the powerful Brahmans in bringing the people back to the worship of the ancient gods.

Khmer kings had all along made elaborate preparations to ensure a happy life after death. And so they propitiated the gods, sought their favour in their efforts to attain immortality. More temples, more monasteries where priests could also add their prayers to those of their god-king. "The king set up his *linga* as a promise of divine favour"—this is the inscription found near one of the temples. Usually the temple in which he had officiated was not used by his successor for he built his own. The deceased king was believed to live on, and special ceremonies and rites were held to invoke the help of the gods for his happiness and immortality. This was an intolerable burden imposed upon the masses, and one which they now looked upon with increasing resentment.

In most Khmer cities the palaces, temples and administrative offices were built in the centre, where a sacred temple mountain was erected to serve as a guardian of this miniature universe. It included an altar dedicated to the gods and givers of life and fertility. The rice fields and cultivated lands were connected by causeways, irrigated by canals, or protected by ramparts which surrounded the city proper.

This pattern symbolized the world enciled by a chain of mountains and the mythical oceans. The temple in the centre represented Mount Meru with its five towers corresponding to the five peaks of the sacred mountain and the terraces rising tier after tier like a series of worlds. It was a ritual compass, the horizontal and vertical axes marking the four cardinal points, the zenith and its opposite. The lesser shrines represented the constellations in their courses.

Temple worship, the residence of the gods, required that the worshippers filed around the building passing through each successive stage of the solar cycle, crossing space in step with time. It was believed that the temple, with its symbolic and mythical associations, and the solemn ritualistic procession of the devotees, ensured the supreme effect of the special sacrifices offered up by the god-king, who passed down to his people the blessings which descended from the mountain.

Temple worship was both impressive and awe-inspiring, Siva, Vishnu or Brahma were worshipped with a blind acceptance of their fearful power, their supreme omnipotence, and the realization by the masses of their own lowliness as they cringed and prostrated themselves before them, but all knew that the reigning king was the re-incarnation of the god, and they worshipped the living being. Yet fear was not the only sentiment; in times of prosperity services of thanks were devoted to god and god-king.

The services were conducted with great dignity, solemnity and the most colourful pageantry. The dark interiors of these massive and forbidding temples were illuminated by the light from hundreds of candles. It was extravagance of course, but there was a magnificence and splendour about it, and evidence of strong religious fervour. The god-kings and the priest cults never underestimated the extent of the unity which a national religion brings to a nation.

The light shone on the gods. Usually it was an enormous bronze, for in this work the Khmers excelled. Vishnu or another of the trinity lay in his sanctuary, decorated with precious stones, metals or coloured enamels. Jewels flashed from his eyes. The belief was widely held that at the end of every cycle the all-powerful god would bring order and peace to a troubled and war-weary world. Sometimes the god rested on a raised platform in the centre of a lake, and a fountain in his navel sprayed streams of water into the air to fall back into the waters of the lake.

The ritual was complicated, lengthy, with the priests performing various rites according to their rank. The Brahmans wore long white coats bordered with gold brocade, and at intervals blew on conch shells. The entire priest hierarchy bore themselves with an air of humility, yet it was not without self-importance, for they were fully conscious of the awe in which they, as intermediaries of the great god, were held by those who knelt before them. But they were submissive and disciplined members of a powerful hierarchy and the ambitious were well aware that there were several steps on the ladder of promotion, and a knowledge of the history and dogma were not the only qualifications required. The chief priest saw to it that seniority received due respect from the subordinates.

The priests were assisted by musicians, precentors and vocalists, who chanted sacred incantations. The choristers were carefully selected, and the training was rigorous. Their voices filled the lofty and spacious temple and the hymns of praise required a pitch and cadence which would interpret faithfully the court poet's inspirations and send the exaltation and love soaring to the gods as well as imbuing the worshippers with a deep and abiding sense of their greatness. And on earth their king was the re-incarnation of the god.

Trumpets, bronze conches, huge drums borne on the shoulders of bearers or fixed in wooden frames and carried, smaller drums and gongs supported the orchestrated choir, or played without it as the procession filed slowly around the temple. The statues of the gods were carried on gold shields under gilded parasols.

It was now the turn of the worshippers. They advanced with flower offerings which they placed on the shrine. All the priests and worshippers hoped that the gods would be pleased by the homage and devotion they had been accorded.

The Khmer's religion was an amalgam of the worship of Siva, Vishnu and Brahman who formed the trinity, and Buddha, particularly the Lokesvara. Brahma was the least fashionable. None of the principal buildings were Bhraman. God-kings were, of course, identified with the trinity and later with the Buddha, but when Mahayanist Buddhism changed to Hinayanist, the cult lost favour.

There appears to have been a deliberate avoidance of sex in Khmer architecture. The people were clearly deeply religious. The numerous temples and idols are sufficient evidence of this quality, but according to Chou Ta-kuan their morals were low. Moreover, they were not prudish, for he also says that mixed bathing in the nude was customary.

The architecture, the statues and bas-reliefs of their temples had to conform to a pattern of sanctity suitable to the religious nature of the building. It is likely that this had the effect of making the sculptors over-modest.

The sculptured goddesses and temple dancers have bare breasts, but are discreetly robed. The male figures, including the Leper King have no genitals. Although a large number of temples were dedicated to Siva, whose symbol was the phallus or *linga*, this was so fashioned that in some cases it is unrecognizable. There are no sex figures on the bas-reliefs or the monuments.

Nothing was allowed to offend the eye in this particular sense. Otherwise, sexual freedom was tolerated, provided that it was not practised in public. Sexual orgies, in the guise of religious rites, were frequent affairs inside the temple precincts, but care was taken to see that this information was not noised abroad.

Geoffrey Gorer, who was convinced of the Khmers' addiction to opium, says*.

opium is, however, absolutely necessary for the comprehension of their art. Khmer art has always seemed strange and alien to European commentators, and the strangeness, in analysis, is caused by the fact that Khmer art is extremely sensual and completely sexless. In the square miles of Khmer sculpture at Angkor, there is not a single sexual figure or group; the very rare nudes are dedicated to Shiva whose symbol is the *phallus* or *lingam*; the *lingam* are stylised out of all recognition, and the decorations as chaste there as anywhere. . . . The chaste Khmer figures are extremely voluptuous, curved and adorned with an obvious appreciation of human beauty, but with no desire. And this peculiar attitude is, I am sure, the result of opium.

He quotes an extract from an American novel *Sailors Don't Care*† which describes the effect of opium. The person concerned "never had such a feeling of power, of supreme happiness in his life . . . beautiful women had thronged about him, smiling and laughing at him, yet there had been no sensation of sex, but only delightful understanding and companionship".

Gorer compares this vision with the pictures of the *apsaras* on the Angkor temple. "These *devatas* and flower garlanded sylphs re-appear endlessly on every wall of nearly every temple; smiling enigmatically . . . seen with such sensual admiration but with no desire, aversion rather-in hieratic dancing poses, kindly and formal and inhuman. Every sanctuary has this sensual, undesired embroidery."

* *Bali and Angkor* by Geoffrey Gorer.
† Published E. Lanham, Paris 1929.

It is doubtful whether the Khmer sculptors were addicted to opium to the extent Gorer believed. This would mean that the drug was used for centuries.

However, to assess the impact of religion upon the Khmers, it is necessary to examine the Hindu trinity and find out how the priests portrayed it. Hinduism was a complex of Vedic rites and pre-Aryan cults. It was based upon the gods Siva and Vishnu. These gods appear to have alternated in popularity. For example, Vishnu was more to the fore in the eleventh and early twelfth centuries.

He was represented as the preserver of the cosmos, the kind and charitable god who presides over the destinies of mankind. At the height of his popularity he was considered to be the most important of the solar deities, regarded as the supreme deity by his followers. He possessed some of the characteristics of Indra and Prajapati. He resides in Vaikrentha, which is his heaven, with his wife Lakshmi.

His physical representation is that of a handsome youth wearing a tall cylindrical mitre, with four hands which hold the *pancha-janya* or conch shell, the *chakra* or wheel or sun disc, a club and a lotus. On his breast, he wears *kaustaba* or jewel Vishnu and the *sirvatsa* or mark of the sacred hair. His *sargna* or bow, and *nandaka* or master of the dance emblem are close by. He is mounted on a *garuda*, the sun bird. Vishnu has numerous titles, some of which are Lord of the Universe, Lord Creator and Governor of All, Lord of Waters.

He is the god who presides over the Churning of the Sea of Milk, both in his physical form, and as Kurma, the tortoise who supports Mount Meru. Vishnu is also seen in cosmic sleep between the creation of two worlds. Lakshmi is also a goddess of prosperity and fortune.

Many *atavars* or incarnations were attributed to him. The ten most popular are tortoise, Buddha, fish, boar, dwarf, Brahmin, Rama, Krishna, man, lion and Kalki or the *avatar-yet to-come*. The Khmers accepted that the god passes through a series of reincarnations in order to satisfy men's desires, or to offset some great evil in the world. They were particularly partial to the *atavars* of Indra and Rama. Some authorities maintain that in the boar and tortoise *atavars* he raised the earth from the bottom of the ocean. The view was widely held that his divine spirit had been assimilated in a human and supernatural form. Vishnu divides his spirit into male and female; the male passing down to Rama and Krishna, and the female into Sita and Radha.

The *Ramayana*, or the life story of Rama, was written in Sanskrit during the second century before Christ and was later translated into Indian languages. It is one of the most popular religious writings in that country. Briefly, it relates the story of the Indian prince Rama who married Sita. A usurper seized his throne, and Rama wandered in the jungle living the life of an ascetic with his wife. Sita was seized and carried off by Ravana, the demon king of Lanka (Ceylon). Rama enlisted the help of the monkey king Hanuman, and his many followers. He crossed the sea in an aerial chariot, or by way of the islands known as Rama's bridge, and brought her home with him to share the throne.

A popular reincarnation depicted of Vishnu is that of Rama with his bows and arrows, accompanied by his faithful brother Lakshman.

Indian women today look upon Sita as the ideal of feminine purity and fidelity. Hanuman is depicted in an attitude of devotion before Rama, and is regarded as a great hero.

Siva, the other great Hindu god whose image was built in so many temples in Cambodia is the god of destruction, but also of creation. He is also a sustainer. Saivites, or followers of Siva, look upon all other gods as his subordinates. They hold that death is the mother of life. The Khmers represented only the most benevolent aspects of this god, even if the sculptors did sometimes make him appear fearsome. He was the god of gods, god of nature, learning, dancing, revelry, the arts. His symbol is the *linga*. He is the incarnation of creative energy, particularly of Nature.

He is represented as a fair-skinned young man, with a tall curly chignon carrying the crest of the crescent moon, four arms, an additional or frontal eye. In his four arms he holds his emblems; the trident which symbolizes the thunderbolt, the bow, the timbrel and the club. This third eye possesses such destructive power that the gods are all created and destroyed by a mere glance. He wears the skin of a tiger or an elephant. Serpents twine around his neck which is blue from the poison he drank to prevent it from destroying the world. Siva rides Nandi, a white bull. On his forehead is depicted the crescent moon which is a symbol of his sovereignty. The god has many names. The most common is

Mahaderas. He has no real incarnations although his followers claim him to have twenty-eight. His abode is Kailasa, the sacred mountain, where his worshippers hope to go. The worshippers of Siva are in a majority among Hindus, and all sects worship him as a god of luck.

Saivism, still practised, of course, in India today, is the exaltation of Siva as the Supreme Being, and the merging of the other gods of the trinity, Brahma and Vishnu into Siva.

In early mythology Siva was the Lord of Agriculture. He is a terrestial god, living in the Himalayas or in Benares. At Nataraja he performs the cosmic dance of five movements; creation, preservation, destruction, reincarnation or illusion, salvation or ultimate release.

Another dance, Urahya, demonstrates his amusing competition with his consort Kali, the goddess of destruction. He was acclaimed the victor through being able to lift one of his legs to his head. This action Kali could not emulate, either from modesty or lack of the necessary agility. His dances are often represented in Cambodian art where he is shown encircled by fire. In his cosmic dance, he is depicted as vanquishing evil. In a dispute with heretical *rishis* he deprived creatures of their black magic. These included a fierce tiger, a snake which he wound around his neck and a wicked dwarf. He crushed them beneath his feet, and continued his dance.

His wife Parvati, or Daughter of the Mountain, is often portrayed sitting on his knee, as in the scene where the god is seated on the top of Mount Kailasa which the thousand-headed Ravana, ambitious and aggressive, endeavoured to overturn.

Brahma, the last of the Hindu trinity, never attained much importance in Cambodia. He is depicted red in colour with four faces and mounted on the *hamsa* or sacred goose. A fifth face was was burnt off by Siva for disrespect. He controls a quarter of the universe with each face. According to the Ramayana, he created the world and raised the earth. The Mahabharata says that he came from the navel of Vishnu or from the lotus growing from the navel of Vishnu. The Saivites believe that Rudra created Brahma.

His followers believe that the world will eventually be consumed with fire, after which it will be recreated by God repeatedly, after 100 years of Brahma days, each one of which is almost an infinity in itself, after which the whole universe and the gods themselves will be resolved into the first age. Brahma is represented as holding in his four hands a sceptre, a string of beads, spoon, water jug, and the Veda. His consort was Sarasvati with whom, as the father of men, he had incestuous relations.

Indra, another god, was the great magician, the god of the firmament, who rode his white elephant and was chief of the Lokapala or regents of the world who frequently appear at the four cardinal points of the temples.

The *naga* or serpent gods of the lower regions were held in awe, partly because they were identified with the water spirits and also because of the legend which stated that the Khmer kings claimed descent from the union of the Indian prince and the daughter of the Kings of the *Naga*, who gave the soil of Cambodia as dowry after first drinking the water that covered it.

There were numerous minor gods who dwelt within the sanctuaries; gods associated with the demons, and easily distinguished by their benevolent facial expressions as opposed to the ferocious grins of the latter.

Like their god-kings, the Khmers were terrified of Siva, Vishnu and to a lesser extent Brahma. There was a compulsive desire to please them. It is possible that the gigantic stone faces with their stern, even cruel expressions, helped to inspire this fear. Like their rulers, they had an obsession with death. The priests taught them that there were several forms of Hell in the hereafter, and this struck terror in their minds. Hell, with the most excruciating tortures, awaited those who sinned, and what greater sin than a crime against the god-king or his priests. Disobedience, defiance of a royal command, there were punishments on earth and after for such wickedness. The sculptors depicted Hell in the most gruesome scenes. Heaven was the wonderful state of eternal happiness. A dream of the joys that awaited them or the nightmare of the suffering which could well be their lot. Those were two powerful agencies in consolidating the power of the god-king in the belief in all powerful gods and the priests of the trinity. They were most effective in disciplining the masses.

However, the population gave the sweat of their brows to the service of these gods. They paid for the magnificent temples, the thousands of priests, the costly jewels, the precious stones. Surely thousands must have asked themselves—what have these gods given me?

The priests were too far away from them in thought and

rapport. The spirit world, the rain and river gods, were close to them as they are today, for they gave them their staple diet of rice and fish.

It was here that Buddhism triumphed right from the arrival of the saffron-robed, shaven-headed monks who tramped the streets with their begging bowls. Their success is remarkable when it is realized that there was no Buddhist Church such as, with its hierarchy of priestly ranks and titles, existed in the countries of the West centuries before the followers of the Enlightened One made their tremendous and lasting impact upon Cambodia. The temples were dedicated to the gods of Siva or Vishnu, with only a few to Brahma. There were no Buddhist temples until Jayavarman VII built them, and as his form of Buddhism was Mahayanist, it clashed with that taught by the Buddhist monks.

The great mass of the Khmer population were followers of the trinity as their ancestors had been for centuries. It was the order of life as it was in death.

The Buddhist monks had a very simple story to tell and it was one that was easy to understand. They did not attack other religions or cults. They told of their own way of life, and of millions like them. It was to follow in the path of the Enlightened One. He was an ordinary man without additional arms or eyes. And everyone could emulate his life since he was one of them.

This man they told the Khmers about was Gotama. He had been born during one of those frequent periods when no one was surprised if a young man gave up a life of pleasure and left his home and family, wealth and position to live the life of a beggar or a hermit. This one was a prince with a wife and a small daughter, and was just under 30 years old when, with five of his closest friends, with whom he had been discussing his views, he wandered into the forest.

For five years he travelled, and during this time he established a reputation for asceticism, hard work, tirelessness and compassion for the sufferings of others. His faithful followers stayed with him. His brilliant, eloquent preaching attracted the curious from a wide area, and they followed him from place to place. He had established a great reputation, not only as a preacher, but also as a wise man. However, his tremendous and sustained exertions led to a serious illness. When he recovered, he decided to modify his rigorous mode of living and lead a hard but less strenuous life. He called it The Middle Way, and this expression has been one of the tenets of Buddhism throughout the twenty-five centuries of its existence. The reason behind this wise move was that he realized that a life of extreme self-denial and continuous exertion would bring him to an early death, in which case the whole purpose of his mission would have been in vain.

By any standards this easier life he had in mind was hard enough. Absolute chastity, and only one meal a day, which would usually consist of curry and rice taken before noon, then only liquid until the next meal.

He expected his original five followers to agree with his decision, for they had frequently expressed concern at the severe strain to which he had subjected his constitution. Unfortunately, they were fanatics who could not see the practical side of his suggestion. They wanted him to live, but to continue to deny himself all but the bare necessities of life. They reproached him bitterly and being unable to bring him round to this viewpoint they left him.

He set off on his own, and in the course of his travels he rested one night under a pipal tree. This was later to be known as the Tree of Knowledge, or in Singhalese, the Bo Tree, and it has been replanted from its own seeds down through the centuries. He had vowed that he would never get up until he had found the answer to the questions which had tormented him all his life. In the early hours of the morning he slipped into a trance, and in that state of mind the questions were answered. At last he understood the mystery of life, with all its sorrows, frustrations, pain, joy and ultimate deliverances. He visualized the path which led to final release from pain and sorrow, freed from the desires which tempt and drive one through cycle after cycle of meaningless existence, to be absorbed into the wonderful peace of not-being; in short from Karma to Karma to the final and complete state of happiness—Nirvana.

He was satisfied beyond doubt that he now had the way to the knowledge all men desired, and he took upon himself the title of Buddha, the Enlightened One, and Tathagata, the Perfect One.

Buddha now returned to the spot where his five comrades had deserted him, and followed their trail. He found them in the deer park of Benares. When they saw him they tried to get away, for they had already regretted their action, but he forced them to confront him. They stared in amazement at his face for they had never seen such a look of serenity and wisdom upon it. They saw the greater light which shone from it. and simultaneously they cried, "Brother!"

He acknowledged their salutation and homage with the words: "Oh, monks, address not the Tathagata as Brother. Tathagata is the Holy and Supreme Brother".

Then he preached his now famous sermon. He told of the new way of life which had been revealed to him. It was to the effect that life consisted mainly of suffering, and that his enlightenment under the Bo Tree was that the cause of human suffering was ignorance, that everyone was always demanding satisfaction for something we call self, yet there is no self. We are all transitory formations. The concept of self, selfhood, and the ignorance that accompanies it must be set aside. "Craving for the gratification of the passions, craving for a future life, craving for success in this life"—all this causes unhappiness. The mind must be free from superstition through the stern discipline of our own wills, through love, to mix in the world and be a humble and contented part of it. In this way, peace and happiness could be obtained. He gave eight rules, the observance of which would bring salvation:

1. Blessed are they who *know* and whose knowledge is free from delusion and superstition.
2. Blessed are they who speak what they know in a kindly, open and truthful manner.
3. Blessed are they whose conduct is peaceful, honest and pure.
4. Blessed are they who earn their livelihood in a way that brings hurt or danger to no living things.
5. Blessed are the tranquil who have cast out pride, ill will, self righteousness, and put in their place love, pity, and sympathy.
6. Blessed are ye when ye direct your best efforts to self training or self control.
7. Blessed beyond measure, when ye are by this means unwrapped from the limitations of selfhood.
8. And blessed, finally, are they who find rapture in contemplating what is deeply and really true about this world and our life in it.

He made no reference to God, but to moral order, which only an omnipotent and just deity could bring about. He told them that every good act brought merit, every evil one retribution.

There could be no forgiveness, no redemption. A thought, an idea follows the same pattern as living things. It is born, it dies and decays. There is an inescapable moral law which is enacted whatever is done with body or mind.

He denounced the ritual as pomposity of monks, their self importance and pageantry—as well as the sacrifices. Those of his followers who preached in Angkor must have found their audience particularly receptive to this view. He advised a close contemplation of Reality and the application of private prayer. The trances of contemplation into which he projected himself and trained his followers to copy were not in themselves prayer, but were something often prayed for. This was resignation, an acceptance.

Dr. Luang Suriyabongs, a well-known authority on Buddhism whom I knew for years, summed up its basic principles briefly:

Buddhism foregoes the idea of a God-Entity and the theories of a permanent individual soul. The whole universe is in a state of flux ... all is subject to the universal law of Karma. The whole universe and all life in it is bound to the circle of Life, to the Circle of Re-birth. Thus, a man is born according to his past Karma which, together with his present Karma, will determine his future existence. His past Karma cannot be undone, and whatever Karma has been committed must inevitably run its own natural course until the effects of his will-actions have exhausted themselves, which may occur either in his life or in some future existence. . . . Buddhism thus places the fate of man squarely in his own hands. . . . He can, by avoiding evil and by doing good, and by purifying his heart from greed, ill-will and delusion, create a better Karma for himself which will lead to his salvation, or he can use his power to do evil, which will inevitably create bad Karma, and bring still further suffering, and will retard his salvation from the "Circle of Re-birth".

The keynote of this new teaching, and the main reason for its success was tolerance. No one must interfere with a man's path towards his ultimate end. Every man must be free to choose his own religion, to work out his own salvation.

He told them not to believe everything just because of what the teachers or priests told them. Whatever accords with your own experience, and after thorough investigation agrees with your own reason and is conducive to your own welfare and to that of all other living things, that accept as truth and live accordingly.

It is not difficult to imagine the effect of these views upon the Khmers. These quiet, soft-spoken, saffron-robed monks were debunking the existence of a god-entity, and the priest hierarchy with its extravagance, its trappings of office, both of which were the main pillars of Khmer civilization and the chief agencies employed in the subjugation of the masses. The shedding of blood was wrong, and here again this was at variance with the policy of the god-kings for the empire had been built and maintained by wars of aggression.

One remarkable and commendable characteristic of the god-kings was that they accepted Buddhism freely from the inception of the empire, and even encouraged its spread throughout their domains. If ever a country deserves an honoured place in history for its religious tolerance and freedom of worship, it is Cambodia. Its outstanding record in this attribute has never been surpassed, and is possibly only equalled by that of its ancient enemy, Siam.

George Groslier,* the eminent French historian and authority on Khmer civilization gives a fair and concise judgement on the attitude of certain famous Khmer kings towards Buddhism.

He states that Buddhism, which in the Mahayanist form penetrated Cambodia early, had followers and temples throughout its history, and that the Saivist kings, Yasovarman, Rajendravarman, Jayavarman V, Suryavarman II† *"et les ministres puissantes favoriser le Buddhisme et ériger à la fois des lingas et des statues de Buddha."*

It is possible that the benevolent attitude adopted towards Buddhism by the Khmer kings was due to the particular form of the creed which was practised at the time, There were, as there are today, two forms. One is Mahayana, or Buddhism of the Greater Vehicle, and Hinayana or Theravada, of the Lesser Vehicle. Historians and experts on Khmer civilization and culture are divided as to which of the two kinds was first introduced into the Khmer kingdom. The actual form is important for this would account for its acceptance in the land by the god-kings. George Groslier‡ claims that it was Mahayana. Madeleine Giteau § supports Hinayana.

It may be useful to explain the basic differences. Theravada originated in Ceylon, and was the doctrine of Thera. It did not

* *Recherches sur les Cambodgiens*, by George Groslier.
† Suryavarman II was a Vishnu god-king.
‡ *Recherches sur les Cambodgines*, by George Groslier.
§ *Khmer Sculpture and the Angkor Civilization*, by Madeleine Giteau.

support the cult of the god-king. Consequently Jayavarman VII was not in this sense a Hinayanist or Theravadist. That he practised many of the compassionate teachings is beyond doubt, and his unswerving belief in the cult of the god-king which was stronger than that of any other Khmer king in history is explained by a megalomania which was a form of madness.

The followers followed strictly the teachings of the Buddha and believed in only one path to salvation, which was the three cardinal principles, the Buddha, his law, and his community.

It adhered to the Pali scriptures and to the ideal of self purification leading to Nirvana through contemplative and moral effort. The monks regarded temples as places where worshippers could pray. This precept was followed after the death of Jayavarman VII when for the next 300 years very few temples were built. Wood or wood and brick buildings were erected as Buddhist monasteries and housed only one shrine, that of the Buddha, before which the people knelt and prayed. Theravada Buddhism was at that time, and over a century before, the religion of the Siamese, and there is little doubt that it had a profound effect upon the Khmers for their monks brought it with them from over the border, and the Khmer Buddhist monks accepted them as belonging to the great fraternity of the saffron robe.

It was a simple, uncomplicated faith to follow and it made a strong appeal to the masses. Yet there is no record of any conflict between the followers of one form or the other. A large number did not consider that the differences in dogma, ritual or beliefs to be of sufficient importance. That they were all followers of the Enlightened One was the guiding principle.

The Mahayana school as founded by Nagarjuna required deep piety. It gave its followers several forms of Buddha, and introduced *bodhisattva*, or one who yielded his place in the line for deliverance to be of service to others. A *bodhisattva* was therefore one who was in the process of becoming a Buddha. They exhorted the faithful to be true to the teachings. Their intercession was invoked by those who hoped to join them in Nirvana. Critics of the Mahayana maintain that its immediate effect was to restrict salvation to a few. Clearly, this philosophy would have been regarded with favour by the god-kings. In effect, it was not so far away from their own life after death. They themselves would be united with the trinity, and the Mahayanists only would attain their heaven. The Mahayanists claimed that they were merely demanding strict piety and purification as a necessary condition of entry to Nirvana.

There was *avalokitesvara*, a merciful god who watched their sufferings, and was referred to as 'the Lord who watches from above'; and *lokesvara*, who because of his mercy and goodness was given the title of 'Lord of the World'.

Mahayana was at its height towards the end of the twelfth century. Then Theravada came in to grow steadily until, by the end of the thirteenth century, it was the more popular. Then its numbers increased enormously. It had come to stay.

The change-over appears to have been accomplished without difficulty. The Mahayanists adapted themselves to the new form. It is possible that as the image of the Buddha was paramount and his monks outnumbered all others, they, too, had a desire to belong.

However, the most exhaustive study of all available records fails to reveal any evidence that the teachings of Buddhism had any effect upon the hordes of slaves. In the appalling conditions in which they existed they did not accept their present lives as a transitory state. For them, there was no hope. It has never been easy to reason with starving people. They want immediate relief. They pleaded for food, a life without the crushing burdens they had to bear. And this, the Buddhist monks could not give them.

They had been told that Siva or Vishnu would give them almost anything and they had asked in vain. The Buddhist monks had not made the same promises. Rather had they given them the same message which Sir Edwin Arnold was to give more eloquently and positively centuries later.*

> Pray not! The Darkness will not brighten
> Ask Nought from the silence for it cannot speak.
> . . . Nought from the helpless Gods by gift and hymn.
> Nor bribe with blood, nor feed with fruits and cakes.
> Within yourselves deliverance must be sought.
> Each man his prison makes. . . .

These miserable wretches could not turn to man or god for comfort. They continued to worship the water spirits and various images which their ancestors had invented or fashioned. The

* *Light of Asia* Book VIII.

(*left*) The temple of Prasat Kravan. (*below*) Entrance to the temple of Banteai Kdei

The temple of Neak Pean:
(*left*) a gateway before
anastylosis, (*below*) the
central sanctuary after
anastylosis

Buddhist monks proselytized and the slaves listened, sullen but cowed. Sometimes several masters would drive their slaves to a central meeting place where they could be addressed by the monks. They were glad to do this for they had been told that by this act they would acquire merit. By earning merit by good deeds they would eventually ascend to Nirvana.

No force or persuasion was used by the saffron-robed priests who preached. It is very probable that they themselves considered that this existence for the slaves was a Karma through which they had to pass in the cycle of birth and re-birth, although with the odds so heavily against them it is difficult to see how they could have achieved piety or merit by their own efforts.

This practice of assembling the slaves never became widespread, and it soon ended. The masters quickly realized that it was useless. The monks, in turn, were forced to agree.

The slaves continued with their forms of worship which the Khmers considered as primitive. But gradually they were, in increasing numbers, finding comfort which was not spiritual but earthly. A crude form of the opium drug was passed round in stealth and gave them the warm, soothing shelter of oblivion.

The Buddhist monks were of the people. In their saffron robes they walked through the streets of the Golden City. Their temples were plain structures, their living quarters built of bamboo, reeds and atap. They were poor, but they were happy, and they made themselves useful in a variety of ways and were well liked.

The cult of the god-king was against the teachings of the Enlightened One, but in successive reigns they had learnt to live with it. It did not affect their teaching. It was perhaps a contradiction, but it was a long-established institution.

The reign of Jayavarman VII gave Buddhism its biggest uplift since the inception of the capital of Angkor. It had the royal blessing of the first Buddhist monarch, although Jayavarman himself followed the more exclusive and ornate Mahayanist school. The greatest social reformer of all Khmer monarchs he could not accept the ideals and practice of equality. Not the living Buddha! Yet this complicated character was sufficient of a realist to allow the monks to continue with the teachings of the Hinayanist school, and made no attempt to interfere or influence them in any way. For they were teaching Buddhism, and he preferred it to the Hindu trinity. The masses yearned for spiritual comfort and peace.

8

Into their primitive homes the saffron-robed monks entered and gave it.

The leaders of the Hindu trinity had always been so much out of touch with the people that they failed to foresee the danger. Buddhism was in the ascendant. Its gentle and friendly teaching was turning the people from war to a longing for peace in the empire and freedom and independence for themselves. And at this time the warlike, ambitious Siamese, Chams and Vietnamese were casting envious eyes at the capital, sending their spies to report on the defences and preparing for a trial of strength. The new philosophy was not conducive to a policy of defiance and aggression which would discourage the enemies.

It took Angkor a long time to die but it was now moving inexorably towards its end. The great building programme died with Jayavarman VII. No more temples were built.

Under Jayarvarman VIII the weaknesses in the defences became more pronounced. His generals pleaded in vain for a new system of fortifications. The king would not listen. He was convinced that no power would attack the capital, and he continued with his efforts to counter the onward sweep of Buddhism, and personally desecrated some of the Buddhist images. This action did not, however, spark off an anti-Buddhist persecution. Its hold over the people was now too strong. Siva replaced Buddha in official worship.

The Siamese now became bolder. A Siamese chief who had married the daughter of Jayavarman VII led a raid into Khmer territory, defeated the Khmer governor of the Upper Menam Valley and founded the kingdom of Sukhothai. This was to be the first Siamese capital city. Under its third king, Ram Kamhaeung, Sukhothai prospered. He was a great general, and after leading some victorious and profitable skirmishes over the Khmer borders, he embarked on more ambitious ventures well into Cambodia. Prince Mangrai, a Siamese prince, conquered the old Mon Kingdom of Haripunaya in the Meping valley, and built the city of Chiengmai. The Siamese king and the prince courted Peking. They sent presents to the emperor Kublai Khan who had conquered the old Siamese kingdom of Nanchao.

Having obtained an assurance of benevolent neutrality and more than a little encouragement from Kublai Khan, the Siamese armies marched on Angkor. King Ram Kamhaeung took the field

and mounted on his war elephant fought a duel with Prince
Chot, the commander of the Khmer army, and was victorious.
The Siamese were eventually forced to retreat but they had
slaughtered a large force of Khmers and created havoc in the
capital. Jayavarman VIII called up all his re-inforcements to drive
back the Siamese. It was general mobilization. Women and children took part in the fighting.

The Siamese must have decided that their campaign was worth
while for they renewed the attack two years later. Kublai Khan
had not forgiven Jayavarman VIII for contemptuously rejecting
the demands from the Mongols for homage. He had further
infuriated the Chinese Emperor by throwing his envoy into a
dungeon, when he had presented the demand in person. He gave
the green light to the Siamese to go ahead. There would be no
interference from mighty China. However, he was interested in
affairs in Angkor and called for a report on the border fighting
and the measures the capital was taking to repulse the Siamese.
Kublai Khan died soon afterwards.

King Ram Kamhaeung's policy of unifying the Siamese was a
brilliant success and accomplished with amazing speed. He
presented himself as the unifying force, and followed the example
of the Khmer kings in having his virtues proclaimed in stone,
although the eulogies were much more modest. One of them
states:

When I grew up to nineteen years of age, Khun Samchon, the ruler
of Chot came to attack Tak. My father went to fight Khun Samchon
on the left. Khun Samchon drove in on the right. Khun Samchon
approached. My father's men fled in disorder. I did not flee. I rode
the elephant Nekbol. I drove in before my father. I fought on
elephant with Khun Samchon. I drove Khun Samchon's elephant
Masmuang to flight. Khun Samchon fled. So my father gave me
the name of Ram Kamhaeung (Ram, the Valiant), . . . If I had any
fruit, sour or sweet, savoury and tasteful, I used to bring it to my
father. If I hunted elephants and caught any I brought them to my
father. If I went to attack a village or town and brought back
elephants, boys, girls, silver or gold, I gave them to my father.
When my father died there remained to me only my elder brother.
I continued to serve my elder brother as I had served my father.
When my elder brother died, I inherited the entire kingdom.

A later inscription, put up shortly after his death, is an eloquent tribute to this remarkable Siamese monarch who must have been a feared adversary of the Khmers.

This one records:

> In the lifetime of King Ram Kamhaeung, this city of Sukhothai is prosperous. In the water there is fish, in the fields there is rice. The ruler does not levy a tax on the people who travel along the road together, leading their oxen on the way to trade and riding their horses on the way to sell. Whoever wishes to trade in elephants, so trades . . . or in horses, so trades . . . in silver and gold, so trades. If a commoner, a noble or a prince dies, let his ancestral home, elephants, family, rice granaries, servants, ancestral plantations . . . devolve to his children. If commoners, nobles or princes have a dispute, the king makes a true investigation and then only does he decide the matter. . . .
>
> At the gateway there is a bell hung up. If any one of the public has a complaint or grievance of body or of mind to put before the king he has only to sound the bell that is hung up. King Ram Kamhaeung, on hearing it, will call him before him for enquiry. The people of this city of Sukhothai are charitably pious and devoted to almsgiving. King Ram Kamhaeung, the ruler of Sukhothai, as well as princes and princesses, gentlemen and ladies of the nobilities, and men and women all have faith in the Buddhist religion.

The earlier victories had won for the Siamese king widespread popularity. The army and the priesthood were behind him. The weakened Khmer kingdom was a rich prize.

SEVEN

Mystery of the Abandoned Capital

King Ram Kamhaeung had thrown off Khmer dominion and was preparing to attack Angkor. A new Khmer king had been enthroned in Angkor. This was Indravarman III. He had received Chou Ta-kuan with courtesy, for he was a realist. He had been a soldier and had married the daughter of the arrogant Jayavarman VIII. Shortly after the marriage he had led a successful palace revolt, deposed his father-in-law and thrown the legal heir into prison.

He did not underestimate the challenge from the Siamese, but in order to discourage further invasions, he did what could be done to strengthen the defences, held manœuvres along the borders in which his Royal Regiment of Elephants took a spectacular part. He realised that his father-in-law had made a fearful blunder in antagonizing Kublai Khan, and he lost no time in sending an embassy to Peking, loaded with presents. The Imperial Court was magnanimous. Face had been restored. He tried to imbue the Khmers with a revival of the warrior spirit, and he deliberately courted popularity. Jayavarman VIII had remained within the palace and temple precincts, except on the occasions of the royal processions. Indravarman walked about the streets talking to all and sundry.

He dismissed the generals he believed to be incompetent, restored pride in the army, and resisted the Siamese attacks with such fury that they were reduced to minor, sporadic skirmishes. With the death of the warrior king Ram Kamhaeung, the power of the Siamese kingdom of Sukhothai declined. Angkor enjoyed a period of much needed peace which lasted for twenty years.

Indravarman did not pursue the anti-Buddhist policy of his father-in-law. He had seen how unpopular it had been. The official state religion and ceremonial continued to be Saivism, but he allowed Buddhists full freedom of worship and gave assistance to one of their monasteries and sacred shrines. In A.D. 1308 he abdicated after a rule of only thirteen years, and students of the Angkor period claim that he did so because he was weary of the temple worship of the trinity, had developed strong Buddhist sympathies, and had decided to seek the peace of a Buddhist monastery where he could lead a simple life of meditation, prayer and service to his fellow men. The court circle and the Brahman set were united in their resolve to maintain the old way of life, and it is known that there were frequent religious disputes. It is possible that he was tired of this too, and decided to escape from the intrigue and corruption.

His successor made little impact upon Khmer history. There are few inscriptions on walls and columns recording his qualities or the qualities of those who followed him, and these stone tributes appear to have been discontinued in the middle of the fourteenth century. Jayavarman Paramesvara encouraged the spread of Buddhism, and not only practised it himself, but endeavoured to get the court to do likewise. The end of the *Davaraja* was in sight. Already royal, court and priest pageantry was losing much of its glamour. More temples were used for the worship of the Buddha.

The Siamese recommenced their invasions. The Khmer empire began to disintegrate as the invaders enjoyed a run of military successes, and annexed outlying provinces which they placed under the rule of a puppet prince. One of these rulers, Prince Uthong, a general of outstanding ability trained his men in the art of lightning assaults. These were dashing cavalry charges with horses renowned for their speed. The territory which he acquired within an amazingly short time became so extensive that he decided to establish a new Siamese capital. The site he chose was a large island in the Chao Phya river, not far from the old Khmer town of Ayodhya.

In A.D. 1350 this city was built. He now had his much-needed base. Ayudhya—there was a slight change in the spelling—was to be the capital of the Siamese kingdom for 400 years. He extended its boundaries until it absorbed the entire territory of the ancient kingdom of Sukhothai, part of Cambodian territory including Louvo or Lopburi, and the neighbouring cities to the east, up to Chantaboon. Southwards, his sovereignty extended to Malacca, westwards to Tavoy and Tennasserim.

A powerful Siamese kingdom was emerging and supplanting

the Khmers as arbiter of politics, even disputes in the region. Worse, the kingdom of the Khmers was now threatened, as was also the entire empire. All this had developed within a comparatively short time. Angkor called the governors of its ninety provinces to a special meeting to draw up plans for mutual assistance. The governors were not fooled. They realized that the capital needed help from them, and was concerned only with its own fate. In any case, the lines of communication were continually being cut, and a determined, powerful aggressor could drive wedges between them and Angkor and turn its forces on whichever one was most strategically placed for an easy victory. For the next eighty years, that is from A.D. 1350 to 1430 war between Siam and Cambodia was almost continuous, although it was mainly between Siam and Angkor .The provinces were quite unable to help.

In 1352, King Uthong, later King Rama Thibodi, decided on a trial of strength. He assembled a large force, placed it under the command of his son, and sent it to make war on Angkor. The Siamese army gained a few minor victories, but when it was near Angkor it was met by a strong force of Khmer troops. The capital had been warned in time, and the Siamese were driven back with heavy losses.

The slave problem was causing the Khmer court great concern. More and more slaves were escaping, and there was an alarming change in the general pattern of their escapes. Up to now they had run off into the jungle, and found their way back to their mountain villages or among friendly tribes. Usually they had been isolated escapes, although sometimes they had gone in pairs. Now they were absconding with some of their employer's possessions. If they were cornered, or if retreat was cut off, they no longer submitted tamely but sold their lives dearly. The old procedure which Chou Ta-kuan described, and which required that they remain motionless while punishment was meted out was disappearing. Cases were reported to the court where slaves had killed their masters, escaped with the loot and were never found again.

The days when vast hordes of them were driven through the Victory Gate had almost vanished. The Khmers were hard pressed to defend the empire against the ever-warring Siamese and the resurgent Chams. The slaves in Angkor were at last a force to be reckoned with. The court's policy was not one of more humane treatment, which might have averted the wholesale desertions and later revolt, but savage repression. Punishment was increased in severity to the point when it was no longer a deterrent. Slaves knew that a cruel death was the penalty for acts which were formerly punished by a flogging, and they became more reckless.

These internal dissensions were reported to Prince Uthong, and he decided to attack Angkor again, hoping this time to defeat the divided capital. Siamese forces besieged the Cambodian town of Phnom Phen which was later to be its capital, and after a year's resistance it surrendered.

Forty years later, the King of Cambodia invaded Siam. He captured nearly 7,000 Siamese, whom he transported to Angkor for road building and the construction of defences, and laid waste the countryside. The following year, King Ramesuen took his revenge. He led a very large army which fought its way right up to Angkor. The Cambodian king, Kodom Bong escaped by boat. Ninety thousand Khmers were made prisoner and taken back to Ayudhya. They appear to have gone quite willingly with their captors, which was not without some significance. Historians state that in this war, fire-arms were used for the first time.

In 1388, the Siamese attacked again. Their generals were amazed at the comparatively light opposition they encountered. Within a few weeks their forces had swept on to the capital and were preparing to take it by storm. King Jayavarman's citadel was strongly fortified. Only a specially selected few, mainly generals and princes, had a plan of the defences; the secret exits and entrances outside the city walls and inside the main city. On the death of one of the inner war council, these plans were entrusted to his successor who swore to guard them with his life.

The kings who followed Jayavarman VII had allowed much that this king had prized so dearly to fall into disrepair, but the defences which he had constructed on such a massive scale were built to last for a long time. The reinforced gates rose 60 feet from the ground and were strong and closely guarded. The towering, thick walls had withstood the ravages of time. The look-out posts commanded a view over a wide area, and all approaches were clearly visible. A system of alarms had been invented and improved upon. The intricate link-up of moats was known only to the inner council. The ramparts were manned in strength. It was an impregnable city, but within its walls conspirators were meeting to plan a betrayal to the Siamese forces. They were convinced that it would be impossible for them to capture Angkor, therefore the Siamese armies had to be allowed to enter. The plotters consisted of generals, ministers, mandarins and farmers. The ringleaders were two mandarins and two Buddhist abbots. They represented a strong body of opinion which was in favour of ending the seemingly endless wars and the oppression by the god-king cult which the court was trying even now to revive.

It is unlikely that they considered themselves to be traitors. They knew that they could count upon a large measure of support among the masses, in whose humble dwellings accounts had been passed down of generation after generation being born into slavery, and who were now cursing the quarries when they passed them, and spitting hate at the king's tax collectors.

The conspirators looked upon the Siamese more as deliverers than as enemies, and believed that thousands would follow their lead. They had not reckoned on the opposition of large numbers whose special privileges depended upon the favour of the god-king.

The conspirators knew that the peasants and slaves outside the city walls had been deserting to the Siamese. They also knew that the followers of what was known as the Intellectual School—the leading sculptors, writers and actors—were coming out strongly in favour of a Buddhist state and did not share the views of the war party which wanted a continuation of the hostilities. The Siamese were Buddhists. The Khmers yearned for peace and the freedom to follow the teachings of the compassionate Buddha. There must be no revival of the god-king cult.

One of the four ring-leaders, a mandarin of the first degree, belonged to the Supreme War Council and accordingly possessed the plans of the defences. With the others he prepared a scheme by which some posts could be neutralized, others weakened, while large Khmer forces would be sent to protect points from which there would be no invasion. It was a master plan, for King Jayavarman had profited by the lessons learnt at such appalling cost by the Cham invasion, and had constructed huge defence works.

The leaders moved with the greatest caution. They knew that if the plot was unmasked all would die a fearful death. The siege continued for six months, and then one night the four slipped out of the capital and made contact with the Siamese commander-in-chief.

A month later, during which time the Siamese had summoned large reinforcements from Ayudhya, they mounted an all-out assault on the capital. Simultaneously, the conspirators rose up. The regiments loyal to the king fought with great heroism, but the key positions had been taken over in accordance with the plan agreed upon between the conspirators and the Siamese commander. For some days the fighting raged, and then all resistance ended. Angkor Thom had fallen once more. This time it had endured a siege of seven months. It is alleged that a leading Khmer general had said, before dying from his wounds, that Angkor was bound to fall sooner or later; it was too close to the fighting Siamese. But like his brother officers he had shouted, "Treachery!" when he had found entire posts abandoned, and Siamese war canoes being rowed swiftly and unmolested to landing stations.

The victorious Siamese robbed the capital of priceless treasures which they packed into invasion barges to be sent to Ayudhya. They also deported thousands of Khmers, but again a large number went without any show of reluctance. A puppet prince was installed in Angkor. The Siamese were sure that they had subdued Angkor for a long time. This prince, Sri Suryo Phawong, was forced to take his orders from the redoubtable Siamese general Phya Jai Narong. He was weak and vacillating and incapable of restoring order out of the chaos which now prevailed in Angkor.

The Siamese forces did not remain long enough in Angkor to consolidate their victory. In the light of later events, this is surprising. There are several reasons for their early departure. The three senior generals were uneasy over their prolonged absence from Ayudhya. Angkor had fallen through intrigue and treachery. Khmer princes and nobles had been slaughtered or had gone into hiding with those who had held prominent positions at court. If all this could happen in Angkor in spite of the sacred but fearful oath of loyalty which was required of all officials, a similar situation could not be ruled out back in Ayudhya. Runners had been dispatched to announce the glad tidings of their victory. This would thrill the masses, but would arouse jealousy among the influential mandarins.

Then they believed that Angkor was beaten. While in some sections of the capital the Khmers had fought desperately, in others there had been a speedy surrender followed by what amounted to a welcome. The invaders had not recovered from their surprise. This was news which would astonish the court at Ayudhya. The reports which had reached the king that the Khmers were decadent had not been believed. Siamese generals had been divided. Some had maintained that these stories had been deliberately put out to ensnare Siamese troops; others believed them, and had had their way. Now that they had been proved right, they naturally expected a delighted king to demonstrate his gratitude.

The generals were also influenced by the conduct of their soldiers. After besieging the capital for seven months, the pleasures of victory were undermining the discipline. Ayudhya was a very young capital and its existence and development depended upon a strong army, trained not only in the art of war, but in obedience, endurance and hardship. The Siamese commander-in-chief decided to withdraw his forces. He was well content. The Khmers were incapable of launching any fresh wars of aggression. He doubted if they were in a position to resist a renewed Siamese attack. They were taking back with them a large amount of loot as well as Khmer captives. It would be acclaimed in Ayudha as a most brilliant campaign.

A few of his advisers demurred. They pointed out that there were numerous caches of treasures all over the capital which they should make the Khmers hand over to them, but he was adamant. Such action would delay the return to Siam. The prisoners could be interrogated at leisure and they would divulge all the information required. Then, armed with this and any further knowledge the king required, they could once more invade. He pointed out that each fresh war should send the soldiers home victorious, but with the rich prizes of their successes. Consequently, Angkor escaped comparatively lightly compared with her appalling fate in subsequent hostilities, and the Siamese soldiers marched home to a triumphant welcome.

A wave of nationalism swept Ayudhya. The city was rapidly becoming the capital of a unified and powerful kingdom which possessed rich natural resources. However, there was a temporary setback when the Siamese usurper was murdered and the Khmers regained the throne. The new king set up his court at Caturmukha, the 'city of four faces', and sent no less than three missions to Peking in one year, hoping that China would dissuade both the Chams and the Siamese from attacks on the Khmer empire. But China was pre-occupied with her own internal problems.

A bloody feud now developed in the royal family which had now returned to the former capital at Angkor. On the death of the king, his brothers Sri Raja and Tieraja fought for the throne. Tieraja killed his brother and became king, only to be dethroned in a *coup* led by his own son Dharmaraja.

The cult of the god-king was in its death throes. Only a brilliant and gifted king could save it, and the last few monarchs had been mediocre. Royal processions were not held as often as a quarter of a century ago. Almost the entire population, including the much privileged court circle was Buddhist. This was a unifying force, but it was one of total renunciation, and this was as destructive to the leaders of any aggressive power as the belief in the cult of the god-king was to the whole country at that time.

George Coedès accurately sums up the position as it was in Angkor in those days. In his book *Pour mieux comprendre Angkor* he says: "From the day when the sovereign ceased to be Siva descended to earth, or the living Buddha as Jayavarman VII had been, the royal dynasty failed any longer to inspire the people with the religious respect which enabled it to accomplish great enterprises. Under the threat of the anarchical spirit of the Sinhalese Buddhism his prestige diminished, his temporal power crumbled away and his god-king was thrown down from the altar."

About the year A.D. 1428 there was a period of crisis in Angkor. There were disputes at court; wholesale desertions to the Siamese forces, the news of whose victories was spreading throughout the disintegrating Khmer empire, and among those states which had already broken away. The rice yield had declined alarmingly, due to the grave weaknesses in the once splendid system of irrigation. Dry rice cultivation could not make up the deficit. The Chams on the one front and the Siamese on the opposite were making sporadic raids with impunity. An effort had been made to buy off the more aggressive and powerful of the two, which were the Siamese, but Angkor had reached that state of impotence when the Siamese could choose their own time to launch a fresh onslaught.

The mighty Mekong, which for centuries had given Cambodia a more than adequate supply of water, which had been diverted by an ingenious irrigation system of channels and waterworks into storage tanks, overflowed and the flood waters poured over the land. The Khmers flung themselves into the work of conservation, and built emergency dams. Jayavarman's ruinous policy of deforestation, by which trees had been cut down in large numbers, was responsible for the soil losing its tightening, drainage, and absorbent qualities.

The news of these disasters, some successive, some concurrent was reported to Ayudhya by the well-trained spies. With one eye on the Chams, the Siamese went ahead with their invasion plans. They worked with feverish haste to assemble the largest army that had ever fought in their campaigns. It was equipped with fire rockets which could land with deadly accuracy, rapid arrow shooting contrivances, war elephants and some firearms.

And then they hurled their might against the capital. They were not so much interested in what was left of the Khmer empire as in seizing the capital and taking possession of its riches. To them it was the symbol of the most brilliant civilization of South-east Asia. Accounts had been circulated all over the region of its almost inexhaustible wealth. It was said—and with truth—that even the hundreds of concubines were adorned with collars of rubies. The transparent dresses of the numerous dancing girls were secured with clasps of gold. Ropes of pearls encircled their necks to droop between their breasts. In the royal palace, the floors were of silver. The *apsaras* or temple dancers, chosen for their beauty and trained to be graceful and seductive danced steps of abandon and twisted their half-clad bodies in sensuous movements, or broke their hymens on golden *lingas*; and although only the court circle and the privileged inner ring were allowed to join in these sexual excesses at which their prowess was acclaimed—although it was regarded as part of the rites of temple worship and the cult of Siva—the stories of these orgies leaked out. Strangely enough, they were not exaggerated or embellished. A possible explanation is that the informers were the young aristocrats or higher intellectuals whose pedigree was not sufficiently high to be admitted to the jealously guarded circle, and consequently were angry, bitter and frustrated, but not given to extravagant talk which had no foundation.

The nine huge pinnacles of Angkor soared defiantly and proudly to the sky, and from afar they glistened golden in the sunshine. They were beacons, but to the Siamese they were a challenge.

In a matter of days their armies were storming the city of the sun, charging the gates, trying to make fast a series of ramps to cross the moats. For seven months the Khmers fought back tenaciously. Revelry continued unabated in the beleaguered city, the excesses in the temples became more perverted. Temple sacrifices increased. The wrath of Siva, Vishnu and Brahma had to be appeased.

The Siamese forces sat it out. They knew that within the city food stocks were running low. However, the Khmers showed no disposition to come to terms.

After seven months, large reinforcements arrived from Ayudhya, and the Siamese commander concentrated his army on an all-out assault. The battering rams, fire rockets and arrow firing machines inflicted fearful havoc. The Khmers had not been able to make good the damage done to the walls and other lines of defence during the previous campaign. The violence and weight of the offensive proved too much for the weakened defenders. Angkor Thom fell once more to the Siamese, who, working to a plan, commenced a systematic destruction of the city. They also perpetrated fearful and wanton vandalism in the temples, smashing the doors and pillars. Only a few, and these were at some distance from the capital proper miraculously escaped.

Masterpieces in stone were wrecked or taken away; those in bronze were melted down, priceless treasures of intricate craftsmanship in silver and gold were torn out of their setting. Temples which had taken two score or more years to build were devastated beyond restoration in as many days. More Khmers were transported to Siam, where they were put to work on forced labour projects, including the extension of Ayudhya.

It had been an overwhelming victory for the Siamese. They were determined that Angkor should be destroyed. The city was ruthlessly and wantonly laid waste. Then they proceeded to wreck the irrigation system upon which the lives of the inhabitants, the agriculture—in short, the properity of the Khmers had depended for centuries. Their efficiency had been seriously impaired by neglect during the latter part of the reign of Jayavarman

VII and afterwards. The Siamese smashed barrages, booms, and dams, and brought about more destruction in a few weeks than negligence had achieved in a score or more years.

The invasion of Angkor had not been merely a hit-and-run affair. The Siamese remained in the capital for some months. Not all were vandals. Among their leaders were men of vision, who made a detailed study of Khmer civilization. They were deeply interested in its culture and its government, and they took back with them ideas, customs and institutions they could adopt or adapt. They also took the skilled artisans and craftsmen to help to build Ayudhya, which was to be a city of unsurpassed splendour, the 'City of Light' and which was to be entirely destroyed by the Burmese three centuries later. They took back with them thousands of artists, musicians and dancers, whose work and artistry had appealed to them so much while in occupation of the city These dancers displayed their exquisite grace, agility and poetic movement to delighted audiences in a foreign land as they had done in the capital of the god-king, but their physical attractions were not so blatantly displayed. The Siamese ordered that the young lovelies be more adequately clothed.

It was fortunate that the Siamese were enamoured with the Khmer dancing, otherwise it might well have disappeared instead of being preserved until this day.

Back in Angkor, the Khmers took stock of their devastated city. The loss of life was appalling. The masses believed that they had been abandoned. They quickly became apathetic, while at court there were disputes over the succession. The identification of the king with the god and the re-incarnation of the god in the form of the ruling king, both of which had been vital agencies in fostering a belief in divine protection, even invincibility, all this had been shattered. The people began to whisper in their ruined homes among the broken walls of the temples, in the public swimming baths. They had endured so much suffering and hardship over the years that discipline collapsed. There were vociferous demands that Angkor be forsaken. This was regarded with horror and fury by what was left of the ruling classes. To some, it was sacrilege. But the capital was abandoned.

Various theories have been advanced by writers in different countries to account for the disappearance of the Khmers. These are: a fearful plague, a massive uprising by the slaves who killed their masters and escaped with the loot, the effects of the compassionate teachings of the Buddha upon a people exhausted by the heavy strain involved in manual labour, and the astronomical cost of temple worship and the upkeep of the privileged classes. Another theory is that the Khmers were tired of resisting attacks by the rampaging Siamese, Chams and other states, and moved their capital to a site where it could be more easily defended.

The desertion of the capital and the exodus of its population have been shrouded in mystery for centuries, which explains some of the lurid, colourful stories of its last days.

That there has been a dearth of accurate information in the past is an explanation if not a justification of the false reports. Fortunately, new information is continually coming to light, thanks to the brilliant research carried out by the École Française d'Extrême-Orient and the Angkor Conservancy. Work of outstanding importance has been achieved by George Groslier, Bernard Groslier, George Coèdes, Philippe Stern, Paul Mus, Henri Marchal and several others.

Khmer language inscriptions which have been discovered quite recently prove that there were small Khmer communities living under a kingship near Angkor, towards the end of the sixteenth century, after which period they appear to have scattered. It appears highly probable that the Buddhist monks never left the ruined capital. They may have had few followers, but they must have tended their monasteries, if perhaps as a pilgrimage, for when the ruins were discovered their temples were in the best state of preservation. These silent saffron-robed figures and their descendants flitted in and out of the unyielding jungle for centuries, worshipping the Buddha.

There is, however, some conflict of opinion concerning the first fifty years after the fall of Angkor. H. G. Quaritch Wales' fascinating book *Towards Angkor* gives us food for thought. He says: "Yet in our encyclopædias and histories . . . one will search in vain for this far flung empire or its noble founder . . . the very fact of such an empire ever having existed is scarcely known, except by a handful of Oriental scholars."

H. Churchill Candee, who has made an exhaustive study of the ruins of Angkor accepts the disappearance of the Khmers as sudden and says in his book *Angkor the Magnificent* that after a "few score years Angkor was forgotten", and there is much that is true in this judgement.

Bernard Groslier in his book *Angkor Art and Civilization* says:

At the beginning of the fifteenth century the Khmer kings were forced to abandon Angkor, which was razed to the ground, and amid whose dead stones they continued to reign as ghosts. Confined to the central provinces, its capital thrown back first to Lowek and then to Phnom Penh and Udong, Cambodia sank to the level of a third-rate Power, a vassal of Siam barely mentioned by European writers later than the sixteenth century. In the end it would have completely vanished from the map, partitioned between Siam and the Annamites who had settled in Cochin-China after the eighteenth century, had not the French Protectorate come to the rescue at the eleventh hour.

Angkor died, and the separated western parts of the Khmer empire passed to Siam. But not the entire empire of Jayavarman VII. Its eventual disintegration was to come later. There were several reasons for the scene of utter desolation which greeted the Siamese armies when they returned in quest of more plunder, but it was later than the generally accepted term of one year, although the actual date is of far less significance than the fact that the Khmers did abandon their celebrated capital very shortly afterwards.

When the Siamese besieged Angkor it had a population of approximately one million. Thousands were deported or killed, but, even allowing for these heavy casualties, this still left a large number. The Siamese had been thorough. Shipping had been destroyed. Practically all means of transport had been wrecked. The fear of the unknown was deep rooted. The peasants were terrified of venturing into unexplored territory, but their fear of Angkor was just as great. The old and the very young were burdens to the able-bodied and they were left to fend for themselves. Vast numbers banded together, prepared to brave the rigours and perils of the jungle, which included the ferocious wild beasts as it does today. There is no record of what happened to those who belonged to the first exodus, but it is not difficult to imagine their fate. The pride of the Khmer army—the Royal Regiment of Elephants was now no longer a defence, still less a striking force.

The court remained in Angkor for a year or two, and made a

9

concentrated effort to repair the irrigation works; but it was a herculean task, far beyond their now slender resources. The population had to be fed. Dry rice cultivation was practised on a much wider scale, but the soil had already been exhausted as a result of these drastic measures. All over the capital and in the remnants of the empire, a slash and burn process was adopted out of expediency. Vast clearings were hacked out in the jungle, fired, and crops planted, but it was soon realized that this method was totally inadequate.

Before the court could launch a massive drive to repair part of the network of the irrigation system, the stricken capital was hit once more by devastating floods. Barrages, dams and dykes were too severely damaged to resist the oncoming waters, which submerged fields and rose higher and higher until they swept away the piles on which the houses were built and rose to the terraces of the temples. The death toll was tremendous.

When they finally receded and some semblance of life returned to Angkor, a fearful epidemic later swept the city. This was the dreadful scourge of malaria. The germs had bred abundantly in the stagnant pools. It is said that the court of astrologers, which was composed of high ranking Brahmans, had exhorted Jayavarman VII to strengthen and extend the ingenious hydraulic system which he had inherited and which for centuries had been the major force in the building of the empire, but he brushed aside their pleas. There was plenty of time, he argued. Nothing could be permitted to impede his building programme. To make matters worse, as Buddhism continued to reach out into the homes, and its teachings were followed, the mosquitoes multiplied because Buddhism forbade the taking of life.

The danger of floods in South-east Asia has never been far from the minds of the government and farmers. There has always been an air of mystery about the mighty Mekong, especially in Cambodia, where it is often referred to as the 'king of rivers'.

The Mekong, which rises in the great mountains of Tibet some 1,500 miles away from the capital of Cambodia, winds its course through the southern provinces of China, between Burma and Thailand, along the borders of Laos and on to the sea. The flow of the Mekong is greatly increased by the spring thaw in the Himalayas, and also by the torrential rains of the wet season.

It is not known how many lives were lost through floods and

malaria. It is likely that the latter exacted a far greater toll because the Khmers had lived with floods before the inception of the empire, but we may assume that they were quite unable to take any effective measures against the disease which now raged in the capital. The corpses were swept out to sea, or were disposed of by vultures, wild dogs, panthers and lions.

With the home defences weakened because of these catastrophes there was another uprising of the slaves. This time it was born more out of terror than cruelty. They attempted a mass flight from the capital, and one can understand the feelings of these wretched creatures. Their masters whom they had been taught to regard as supermen, could do nothing to help them to ward off the floods, or save them from the diseases which racked them with pain until death brought an end to their sufferings. Those who had power of life and death over them and had exercised it without hesitation or apparent regret, died as easily as their fellow slaves.

No positive lead came from the court, where the bitter quarrelling over the accession divided the kingdom. The rival claimants to the throne were many. Whoever did control the kingdom could no longer count upon the blind support of the millions. And yet the Khmers could have saved something from the wreckage, even moved more quickly to another capital as they had done before, if they had taken prompt action. They would have at least saved thousands of lives. Unfortunately, there was no leader who could bring about a measure of unity.

In the absence of any strong determined action from the court, the slaves became bold and reckless. Rival bands joined up and then broke away. They swarmed through the streets of Angkor, killing, burning and looting.

Many of the more intelligent ones broke away from the unruly mobs which were destroying what little the Siamese had left undamaged, or were wandering about in a state of stupor from the orgies of drugs and lust, and followed the tracks of the Siamese army in which they hoped to find service. It is probable that they had a premonition that the revolt would be bloody but short-lived, that the ruling classes would win as they always would. Then the revenge would be fearful. Large numbers just lost themselves in the jungle and died of starvation, or from attacks by the wild and ferocious animals.

Eventually the court managed to achieve some measure of

authority and unity. The army launched a punitive campaign, and with their superior weapons, years of training and discipline stamped out the revolt with merciless severity.

For some months the life of Angkor continued, while the court endeavoured to bring order out of chaos and so organize an orderly retreat. It is likely that many considered that such a step would only be temporary, but they were overruled. The pageantry and animation had gone for ever. The city was dead. The king gave orders to leave. Angkor Thom was abandoned.

No capital in history had suffered a more tragic and devastating accumulation of catastrophic blows, but few would have ignored the writing on the wall or profited so little from previous experiences and disasters.

It is not without significance that there is no report of a visit to the ruined capital from an envoy of Peking. China had been interested in the Khmer empire from the sixth century, the days of Funan. The Siamese were flushed with success. They celebrated their victory with festivities and triumphal parades which continued for several days, and there is no doubt that news of these celebrations reached Peking. It is quite likely that the celestial court was concerned and sent emissaries who reported back that Angkor had been devastated beyond repair and that the irrigation system had collapsed.

That the Siamese armies returned is beyond doubt. Hostilities were soon to break out again between the two countries and were to continue for four centuries. That they found Angkor deserted is not surprising. One can imagine the small community which had stayed behind or had strayed back, watching the oncoming Siamese and hiding in the jungle with the Buddhist monks until the invaders had stalked arrogantly through the abandoned streets, surprised and suspicious, then departed.

The Khmers moved quietly and cautiously to Bassack, but fresh floods drove them out and they moved on to set up headquarters near the present site of Cambodia's present capital at Phnom Penh. A royal palace was built with a bell-shaped *stupa* or spire such as one sees today all over South-east Asia. This overlooked the city from an artificial hill as the traditional Khmer temple mountain.

Cambodian history for the next four centuries until her annexation by the French was tragic. There were long periods of civil war, several murders of rival claimants to the throne; and she was forced to resist constant attacks by the Siamese and Vietnamese.

Early in the seventeenth century her armies captured the town of Lovek and put Soryopor on the throne. He promptly proclaimed Cambodia to be Siam's vassal state and adopted Siamese court ceremonial and protocol as observed at that time in the brilliant capital of Ayudhya. This act aroused the fury of the Khmers. The king was forced to abdicate, and his son, later Chey Chetta II, mobilized his armies, declared Cambodia independent and prepared to fight. The Siamese accepted the challenge. Two large forces were sent from Ayudhya. Both were defeated. A third expedition, this time by sea, met the same fate.

A triumphant Chey Chetta endeavoured to rekindle the warlike spirit of the Khmers, but realizing that his armies were numerically not a match for the Siamese in a war of aggression, and not content with the role of defence, he looked out for allies. Help was quickly forthcoming from Hué. Chey married a Vietnamese princess. The wily Vietnamese persuaded Chey to allow large numbers of Vietnamese to settle in Saigon with the result that it rapidly became a Vietnamese settlement. This short-sighted policy was to involve Cambodia in dispute with the Vietnamese for centuries, and it is still an acute problem today.

When he died, his son was too young and inexperienced in affairs of state; moreover he had lived in a monastery for years. His uncle, Prince Outey was appointed regent. However, the headstrong young man defied his uncle and launched an attack on Siam with the object of regaining the former Khmer province of Korat. It failed, and the embarrassed king went to a town near the former and now very sparsely populated capital of Angkor. There he fell in love with one of his uncle's wives, and took her back with him to live in the royal palace. The angry regent stirred up the people against him, and in a palace revolt both king and mistress were hacked to death.

His younger brother, Prince Nou was made king with Outey still regent. On Nou's death Outey installed his own son Ang Non as king, but another son, Chan, with the support of Cham and Malay mercenaries stormed the palace. It was a bloody carnage. The entire royal family in residence, Prince Outey and the ministers were all slaughtered. The victorious Chan then usurped the throne, embraced Islam—he already had a Moslem wife—and changed his name to Ibrahim.

The Dutch East India Company had established a trading post and factory in Phnom Penh, which had flourished since its inception, in spite of tremendous difficulties. The intrepid and indefatigable Dutch had been led to expect favoured treatment from the new king, but in a wave of national fervour he turned on them, massacred the settlement and burnt their ships. The company at once despatched a punitive expedition to blockade Phnom Penh, but Chan fought back with such reckless courage that the Dutch made peace.

However, his star was set. Two of Outey's sons who had fortunately been away from court on a hunting expedition at the time of the palace massacre and had since gone into hiding, now led a revolt against him. It failed, and they fled to Hué where they were supplied with arms and mercenaries. They marched on Phnom Penh and defeated Outey, who fled the country and died soon afterwards.

Outey's son, So, became king and took the title of Barom Reachen II. While out hunting one day he came upon the ancient capital of Angkor. A stone inscription—we are back to them again!—records that it was only a temporary return of the Khmer court. Another one tells us that for the glorification of the Buddha and Buddhism he had restored the huge towers of the temples, built new summits which he had covered with gold, and consecrated a reliquary to his ancestors. Mention is also made of the birth of his son, whom he had consecrated to Buddha at the temple. He refers to this great domain "of powerful spirits and of the companies of his ancestors."

After a few years at Angkor, the Khmers made another of their disappearances, and turned up again in Phnom Penh. Here the king was murdered by his nephew, who made the dead king's widow his chief queen. Apparently this was not to her liking for she plotted with Cham and Malay mercenaries who stormed the palace and murdered him. His successor, Ang Chei, was in turn killed leading a campaign against his brother. Regicide was by now an established custom.

Hué took advantage of the troubled state of the kingdom to exert great pressure on the Khmers to accept more and more Vietnamese settlers; and the king, to avoid further bloodshed, as well as to offset claims from Siam, agreed to accept Vietnamese suzerainty. He abdicated four times and was crowned five, which made the monarchy the laughing stock of south-east Asia. The image of the god-king was indeed buried deep.

Siam did not like the new king and invaded Cambodia to dethrone him, but the king, Ang Em, appealed to Hué for help. The Siamese were repulsed, but the Vietnamese stepped up their price for the help they had given. Hué assumed control of all Khmer coastal territory in the Gulf of Siam.

In 1721, a Siamese army succeeded in defeating Ang Em's Vietnamese forces and marched on Oudong, the new capital. In order to spare the capital from destruction, Ang Em offered tribute to Ayudhya. The Vietnamese were furious at his duplicity and denounced him in scathing terms as 'The Siamese king'.

A period of anarchy in Cambodia now took over. A party of warlike Khmers massacred some Vietnamese. Hué annexed two provinces. The capital was again moved, this time to Lovek. There were more murders in the royal palace. Sometimes the more fortunate escaped to the enemy countries of Vietnam and Siam, where they were given sanctuary.

Towards the end of the eighteenth century, Cambodia was at the mercy of Siam on one frontier and Vietnam on the other, but Vietnam was soon to constitute the biggest danger. Siam was under constant threat from Burma. The dying Khmer kingdom was forced to side alternately with one or other of her old enemies. Angkor was indeed a phantom town.

In 1845, Vietnam and Siam appear to have reached agreement on Khmer neutrality and independence. The object of this new policy was not so much a change of heart as a warning from one to the other against annexing what little was left of the once vast empire.

However, it was an uneasy truce, and France was to step in and absorb Cambodia into her colonial empire, where she was to remain for a century, to emerge a sovereign power with an entity and independence which she might well have lost for all time to her hostile neighbours. If the Khmers found French rule irksome, then at least they were protected at a very critical period in their national history.

EIGHT

Wonder of the World

The sudden appearance of Angkor Wat is a sight which lives on in the memory whether the tourist or pilgrim comes upon it by plane or by road. One stares down at dense jungle, which ends abruptly. In a vast clearing down below, there are the ruins of some 600 temples and other buildings.

The great edifice of Angkor Wat, the glory of Khmer architecture and of its founder Suryavarman II stands out above them all. If journey's end is reached by road, the traveller comes upon a vast moat and a long causeway, and beyond them huge lotus-bud-shaped towers.

It is a spectacle of beauty, wonder and magnificence. One is struck by its sheer enormity. It is 5,000 feet by 4,000 feet. The central block measures 717 feet by 620 feet at the base, and rises to a height of over 200 feet. A tall tower, flanked by a smaller one on either side and connected by galleries supported on pillars, enhances the beauty of the edifice, particularly the entrance which extends to almost 800 feet. An outer enclosure leads to a paved causeway 500 feet long, which is flanked by *naga* balustrades and opens on to a cruciform terrace in front of the temple. This is rectangular in shape and rises in three tiers to a central cluster of five towers. Each of them is surmounted by a lofty pinnacle. This is the gigantic lotus bud shape one sees from afar. Every terrace is surrounded by galleries with corner towers, and stairways with pavilions in between. The central tower on the highest terrace is connected to axial pavilions by galleries supported on pillars, which divide it into four paved courts.

Such is the view from the end of the causeway. To enter the temple proper, one crosses this causeway, which stretches across the huge moat which is really a very large lake. A tribute to the mathematical genius and skill of the builders is provided by the fact that the moat is 200 yards at every point, and the engineering

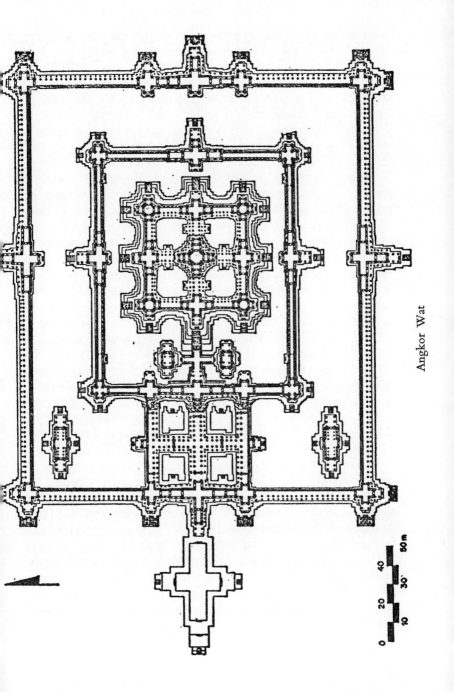

Angkor Wat

error in nearly 4 miles circumference is less than an inch. It is enclosed in masonry. The moat itself is always a beautiful sight with little islands of lotus blooms, water lilies, wild orchids and other wild flowers. No doubt it has been much the same lovely scene throughout the centuries, and ancestors of the modern Khmers have paused to admire it on their way to the temple grounds. It is to be hoped that it was a small measure of compensation for being deprived of the privileges and pleasure of visiting the interior of Angkor Wat except on rare occasions.

While visitors are admiring the perfect blending of the colours, workmen in flat-bottomed boats pole in and out of the masses of white, green, red, blue and yellow, hacking and slashing. This, too, had no doubt been done throughout the reigns of successive kings. Cruel necessity, perhaps, but is obvious that if constant warfare was not waged on this prolific, lush pageant of dazzling colour the entire surface would be covered. Half way along this causeway, two ceremonial flights of steps on either side lead down to the water.

What brilliant scenes in Khmer history had this causeway witnessed! Armies had marched, cavalry had galloped, priests had walked in procession with all the ceremonial of their office.

It continued on to a majestic, five-storeyed and flame-crested triumphal entrance gateway which had been set in the middle of an outer enclosure 600 feet long, which in turn is continued in the form of galleries in both directions and along all four sides. This huge gateway is crowned by three magnificent towers with broken summits.

Beyond the entrance gateway there is another raised gateway nearly a quarter of a mile in length and bordered on both sides by *naga* balustrades broken in several places, with some sections missing. Complete reconstruction would have deprived the edifice of much of its wild beauty and left little to the imagination, and in many cases would have been almost impossible.

Half way along this inner causeway there are two libraries, with square ornamental water lawns in front. They have been built in the parkland and are a pleasing sight, breaking the line of vision from the end of the causeway to the giant towers which confront the visitor.

The balustrades end in the flared seven-hooded cobra heads, which are raised menacingly aloft. They guard the inner sanctuary, and stone lions set on perrons guard the approaches. Inside the sanctuary, temple dancers, nude or semi-nude, and adorned with ropes of pearls danced or performed the temple rites before the god-king, at that time Suryavarman the Great, Suryavarman II, Lord of Lords, King of Kings, Vishnu Incarnate and several other titles.

The visitor has the choice of making the steep ascent to the top terrace or visiting the galleries of bas-reliefs, and then making the ascent. Some prefer to reach the main tower first and then tour the bas-reliefs on the way down. They are an amazing spectacle. So much of it is on an extravagant scale.

Some 2,000 temple dancers, courtesans from the heaven of Indra, carved on walled galleries, pillars, sacred shrines, odd corners have been sculptured in groups or singly, in a variety of graceful and acrobatic poses. Some are high up above the gods and demi-gods to show that they are dancing between an allegorical heaven and earth. Angkor Wat was not only a temple, it was the Golden Meru, the stairway from earth to heaven.

These lovely, smiling and seductive creatures soften the dark grey edifice, its dark galleries, chambers and libraries. They stretch, naked to the waist, along the entire length of the walls of the first and second terraces.

The bas-reliefs are one of Angkor Wat's greatest treasures and outstanding attractions. In the lowest terrace they continue for over half a mile, which gives some idea of the vastness of the temple. Every stone is decorated. The bas-reliefs are about 8 feet high. The whole effect is that of an almost endless tapestry in stone. The subjects are principally religious, of legends and of war.

The scenes from the Ramayana and Mahabharata take up nearly half a mile, and the total number of figures of men, animals and birds has been calculated to be nearly 20,000. There are combats between opposing forces who are mounted on elephants. Hundreds of elephants have been sculptured on the walls, and illustrate some incident from these two legends; warriors fighting from chariots, scenes from the lives of the god Rama and his wife Sita, who was kidnapped by the demon Ravana, armies of men and monkeys. Gods and demons from the caste of the legends of the multi-armed Vishnu. Vast stretches depict Khmer victories on land and sea, naval pageants, victory marches with bands and banners.

The god Vishnu is mounted on a *garuda*; there are invocations to the Hindu trinity, goddesses, guardian deities. One is never far from religious scenes. Hell is made to be terrifying. The condemned are flung into the infernal depths to be tormented by demons. One section is particularly lurid. After judgement there is happiness in heaven, but in hell the demons drag the wretched creatures by ropes passed through their nostrils like water buffaloes. Then they are set upon by elephants, buffaloes, tigers, and suffer the most gruesome tortures. This scene occupied over 300 feet. The effect upon the masses must have been profound.

The god-king was well in evidence. He is depicted surrounded by slaves and soldiers, mounted on a royal elephant, crowned with a royal tiara, setting forth to fight the enemies of Angkor with the blessings of his priest, a high Brahman. A panel on the west section of the south wing is devoted to the more spectacular events in his reign, and are described in the chapter which deals with this king.

The sculptors were fortunate in being provided with a most sensitive, ideal and endless canvas upon which to exercise their talents. This was polished sandstone. They used about 4,000 feet of it. The bas-reliefs decorate eight panels, four of which are over 100 yards long, and three which are half that length. One of these, on the south panel of the east wing, is taken up with the legend of the Churning of the Sea of Milk. Here, the king, identified with the god Vishnu, churns the ocean of fortune to make it produce ambrosia for the welfare of the people. Vishnu is represented in his human form and also as the tortoise Kurma, who supports Mandara which is used as a pivot. The serpent Vasuki is coiled around this mountain and serves as a rope which is pulled by eighty-two gods and ninety-two demons in an effort to extract from the Sea of Milk the elixir which will give them immortality. The Churning of the Sea of Milk was a favourite subject with Khmer sculptors.

Everything about Angkor Wat is on a massive and lavish scale, as if time, expense and labour were of little importance. The bas-reliefs in the majority of cases are executed with exquisite beauty, and the most minute attention to detail, symmetry and proportion. Unfortunately, a large number have deteriorated through exposure, and for some unknown reason others are left unfinished. Perhaps the sculptors became bored, temperamental, or there may have been walk-outs in those days, but this does not explain why a new panel was commenced when work on another was abandoned. In the gallery of the bas-reliefs, all the cross-beams which linked the pillars to those of the outer half vault are broken off. It does not seem likely that this was the work of vandals. George Coedès is of the opinion that it was due to the sinking of the foundations, and this would appear to be the most acceptable explanation. There is no evidence that earthquakes were responsible.

In the parkland and the temple buildings there are over 300 stone lions and an enormous number of monkeys. Their live counterparts frolic merrily among the trees, and it is claimed that lions are not only quite near but have actually been seen crossing the causeway. This is not difficult to believe. It is possible that they have been doing it for centuries. The jungle has, in effect, merely been hacked and slashed back to provide a clearing, but before Henri Mouhot stumbled on the ruins, the wild animals of the forest and jungle wandered in and out of the deserted rooms.

The ascent to the next storey is steep. The steps are in a splendid state of preservation and are very wide. Vaulted stairways climb from terrace to terrace to the summit, where the highest tower rises above the two smaller towers placed on either side.

From these steps a wide variety of views can be admired. In any case, a rest is a welcome break from the upward trudge. A mile or so in the distance one can see the site of the old city. There has been much speculation as to why Suryavarman built Angkor Wat outside the capital. One reason put forward is that he desired it to be isolated. He wanted it to stand alone in all its majesty, for it was his mausoleum. There are grass-grown courts and libraries standing lonely in the corners, broken masonry lying where it has fallen and encrusted with moss.

Another staircase and a courtyard between the first and second storeys provide access to a series of galleries and terraces, and stone rooms with very low doorways. Here it is dark and uninviting. However, there is evidence of the deep religious fervour which has always been a characteristic of the Khmer race. Incense sticks redden and glow, smoulder and die at the foot of sacred shrines or around stone deities. Dark, empty and bare rooms lose a little of their gloom and desolation because of the bunches of flowers which some visitor has placed against the wall or in the corner. It is a common sight to see a man and a woman, usually elderly, kneeling in silent prayer and oblivious of the small procession of callers who walked in and out and did not disturb their vigil.

The ubiquitous Buddhist monk is never far away. The bright colour of the saffron robe helps to brighten the darkness of the rooms. For many, the visit is a pilgrimage. They have walked from distant temples. As far back as they can remember in their particular temple's history, this pilgrimage has been made.* Others live in the temple in the grounds.

The steepest part of the stairway leads to the top terrace and to the sacred shrine which has been built into the lotus bud tower. Here, it is useful to take stock of the giant edifice and study its design, going over one's progress from the base to the summit. I found that this was remarkably easy for the plan unfolds visibly. Angkor Wat is built in three squares, one inner, and two outer ones, but each on a much higher level than the inner. A central group of chambers, and then long and open galleries extend to the right and left all around the square. These galleries have a high limestone wall on the inside and a double square of columns on the outer face.

Each terrace is surrounded by a gallery, interspersed at intervals by corner towers, pavilions, stairways, and axial pavilions. On the highest terrace, the central tower rises high up. It is tied to the axial pavilions by galleries supported by pillars which divide it into four paved courts.

The terraces and towers are connected by ornate galleries and triple aisles, and follow the pattern of the cruciform courtyards below. When one is on the last few steps to the summit the view is magnificent, but, having completed the climb, one is rewarded by a spectacle of breathless beauty. Every tower stands out clearly —for in this country the skies are so often a delightful blue—and is crowned with a soaring pinnacle. Here one can see the intricate, detailed carving of the lotus bud shape. To the ancient Khmers it must have been both awe-inspiring and wonderful. Here was their beautiful bridge from earth to heaven.

These towers possess some remarkable features. They are with-

* Whenever I have visited Angkor Wat I have always encountered large numbers of Buddhist monks climbing the steep stairways or walking from room to room. The remark made by the guide at the Colonial Exhibition in Paris nearly forty years ago comes back to me. "The kings, queens, priests of the Hindu trinity departed. With them, or close at their heels the people moved out. But a few of the large number of Buddhist monks remained. They passed on and others took their place. And so it went on all through the centuries. And so it will continue as long as Angkor stands."

out interior windows or staircases, but they are built in storeys, gradually receding towards the top to form the lotus bud cones which are such an impressive sight when viewed from a plane circling just above them.

That the builders and sculptors were ruled by the ancient religious myths and beliefs in the construction of this and other temples dedicated to the Hindu trinity becomes clear as one contemplates its main features. Angkor Wat, with its walls and moats, central sanctuary, pyramidal temples, *naga* balustrades, reproduced on earth a terrestrial model of part of the heavenly world. Then it conveyed that close connection between the two worlds which promised a future existence. The belief prevailed that the world consisted of a central continent known as Jambudvipa, with Meru the cosmic mountain rising from its centre. This continent was encircled by six concentric rings of land, separated by seven oceans, the outer one enclosed by a wall. The city of Brahma was located at the summit of Meru, and was the abode of the gods. It was surrounded by eight guardians at the cardinal points.

Angkor Wat was therefore a miniature universe, a microcosm, a magnificent replica in stone of Khmer cosmology. Its five towers symbolized the peaks of Meru, the enclosing wall the mountains at the edge of the world, and the surrounding moat the ocean beyond.

The temples carried this representation further. For example, it was believed that Mount Meru extended as much under the earth and the sea as above. Accordingly, the sculptors covered the carved bases of the towers by a second layer which they decorated usually by duplicated bas-reliefs.

Angkor Wat is an architectural masterpiece. It is also the culmination of the efforts of the Khmers over the centuries to produce a monument of outstanding merit to the gods of the Hindu trinity, although later Buddha was to replace them.

It is of interest to note that the earliest pre-Angkor masterpieces go back to the sixth century and they retained their religious motif over the centuries. The buildings, statues, bronzes and sculptures were dedicated to the gods. The Indians brought their religions with them in their quest for fortune or sanctuary in the region of South-east Asia. The Brahman priests accompanied them, but at first in small numbers. It was not long before these increased, for their reception was cordial. These priests belonged to the educated minority. They were the intelligent élite and they wielded enormous influence. In the countries of the region in which they settled they were soon to command respect, for they were usually men of imposing stature, dominant personality who kept themselves aloof so that they remained above their fellow men. This policy paid high dividends. They were acknowledged leaders and held in high regard by kings, who, quick to estimate the extent of their power over the masses, invited them to serve as counsellors.

They were not only men of culture; they possessed a knowledge of medicine produced from the herbs, were familiar with the anatomy, and were well versed in crop cultivation and irrigation. It is not surprising that with all these gifts, these resourceful priests were to make a valuable contribution to the national economy, although how much misfortune and misery this religious era was to bring to the country is a question which has no place here, and is dealt with in another chapter.

The successive courts supported them largely out of self-interest, with the result that the Brahmanic and court spheres of influence were bound up with each other. Thus combined, they presented a powerful force and an authority which was unquestioned. And this authority extended over the building of vast edifices to whichever of the trinity was fashionable at that time. This, up to the end of the twelfth century was Siva.

The legends of this god inspired a large number of bas-reliefs, but the epic poems and generally accepted beliefs became the theme of the Vishnu legends as at Angkor Wat.

In this temple, Vishnu's heaven, he was depicted as merciful and compassionate, despite his mighty power. Deep in cosmic sleep, he creates a new world. His great deeds of chivalry were described in the Mahabharata and handed down from generation to generation. They provided the sculptors of Angor Wat with subject matter as well as inspiration for their sandstone canvases.

The temples were dedicated to the god housed in the sanctuary, but were incarnate in the ruling king. The Brahman priests had fostered this belief right from the start. This meant that the kings in turn were required to erect their own edifices where they were worshipped after death. But to support the cult of the god-king and preserve the hierarchy, the princes and high officials, an exclusive body whose numbers were always strictly controlled, were

(*above*) The Bayon and
(*right*) its outer terrace

The Bayon: one of the stone faces of Jayavarman VII, who believed himself to be the living Buddha

allowed to do the same but with smaller shrines. And so Khmer art was directed to one main purpose which was the immortalization of a few.

The masses did not worship in the accepted sense. It was accepted that they were allowed in the temple to pay homage to the gods.

However, whether it was the era of Vishnu, Siva, Brahma or Buddha, the deity to whom all prostrated themselves was not one of these. That belief had disappeared centuries ago. It was not one of these gods whose images were guarded with such care and ceremonial in their bejewelled shrines before which the priests knelt and chanted and went through their ritual ceremonies, and who was taken out of the sanctuary on very special occasions for the adoration of the masses.

The Khmer knew in his heart that he was paying homage and worshipping the god-king of his time and at Angkor Wat it was its founder Suryavarman II, the living Vishnu.

The Khmer temples have been the target for praise and censure by those with a knowledge of architecture and sculpture. Angkor Wat has escaped comparatively lightly. Some writers have queried what could be described as the wasted space. Sir Sacheverell Sitwell in *The Red Chapels of Banteai Srei*, wrote:

A headlong vertiginous staircase leads from here upward to the central sanctuary or main tower which is in fact an anticlimax for it is no more than a small, dark cell. All the enormous stone mass has no hall of even modest proportions within it. There are but endless galleries and stairs, and except that at least there is a roof overhead Angkor Wat is as useless a structure as Carnac or Stonehenge. It could accommodate great crowds but to no other purpose than their crowding . . . The 'libraries' which are most intricately worked upon stone bases of the utmost elaboration are so wasteful of their own space that they occupy only a small portion of the plinth on which they stand.

However, this may be regarded as a criticism of the layout rather than the architecture. Geoffrey Gorer* who is one of the most trenchant critics of Khmer architecture, and whose views are again quoted in the chapter "Legacy in Stone" finds much that is worthy of high praise at Angkor Wat:

* *Bali and Angkor*, by Geoffrey Gorer, London 1935.
10

The Khmer sculptors, a little before the kingdom was destroyed, had discovered all that anybody could know about the technique of carving in stone, but they had forgotten what to do with the carvings . . . all this learning and experiment culminates in the Angkor Wat, the most perfect building in Angkor, and one of the loveliest pieces of architecture in the world. In architecture, as in all the other arts, the greater the complexity, the greater the effect, provided that the complexity does not overwhelm the unity. In architecture we can distinguish four developments of increasing complexity; first, the simple façade; secondly, the building as a solid of three dimensions; thirdly, the solid building in relation to the surrounding buildings, and lastly, the solid building in relation to the surrounding buildings and the intervening spaces. It is this last qualification which makes Angkor Wat almost unique in the big buildings of the world. Space is treated as a constituent part of the whole. This is the rarest quality of all in architecture, except incidentally in their cloisters the Gothic builders had no conception of it, nor as far as we can see had the Greeks or Romans . . . the cloistered courtyard is perhaps the most successful of all the inventions which have gone to the making of the wat; the proportions are so perfect, the decorations admirably adapted. . . . Perfection once realised in the wat, the Khmer architects appear to have lost their vision. Henceforth it is technique, and especially the technique of the sculptor holds sway.

Bernard Groslier, in his book *Angkor Art and Civilization* says: "All these details, together with the size of the building which bursts into sight at the end of the triumphal avenue and at every embrasure open to the view, contribute to the impressiveness of Angkor Wat. Not unjustly is it the best known Khmer temple and the unique embodiment of the spirit of Angkor, constituting as it does the most perfect expression and unchallengeable pinnacle of Khmer art."

All visitors to Angkor Wat are lost in admiration and wonder at this superb architectural masterpiece. Sir Osbert Sitwell has voiced the feelings of the legions of visitors who have walked in the steps of the Khmers. "Angkor, as it stands, ranks as the chief wonder of the world today, one of the summits to which human genius has aspired in stone."

NINE

Legacy in Stone

Angkor Wat is the great temple, Angkor Thom the old capital. The former stands out sharply against the background of jungle growth. It has been reconstructed and reconstituted in its former majestic beauty, but this clear line of demarcation between building and jungle contrasts violently with the tangled mass of thick roots and branches which is found in the old capital. The jungle has encroached in all directions as if putting forth all its strength to overwhelm the obstructions in its way, determined to reclaim its own. Pierre Loti paints a fascinating picture of this struggle between jungle and stone in his *Un Pèlerin d'Angkor*.

The fig tree is the ruler of Angkor today. Over the palaces and temples which it has practically prised apart, everywhere it unfolds its smooth, pale branches like the coils of a serpent, and its dome of foliage. At first it was nothing but a tiny seed borne on the wind to a frieze at the top of the tower. But as soon as it germinated it worked its roots like threads behind the stones, probing down by a sure instinct towards the earth, and when it reached the soil at last it quickly strengthened and grew with the nourishing sap until grown gigantic, it forced apart, dragged out of line and split open the walls.

This is not to say that a vast area of the capital of Angkor Thom has not been cleared, but there are so many buildings which have crumbled over the centuries, so much stone has fallen and broken, so many galleries and terraces are in need of attention. In some cases reconstruction is either impossible or not worth the labour and expense.

It does not seem feasible that the huge trees whose enormous roots and branches have intertwined around doorways, shattered massive stone faces, burst open ceilings, and prowled along walls as if searching for the weakest point are the original trees, although many visitors like to think that they are. This may have a romantic appeal.

147

In the five centuries which had passed, the same trees could not have survived under the conditions which prevailed in the impenetrable, foetid jungle. Some had lost the fight, for the temples had been the victors; some had merely disintegrated through age, and others had grown upon them. And so the cycle had continued until Henri Mouhot's discovery had led to the monumental work of jungle clearance.

Visitors to Angkor, as well as writers describing their impressions, are inclined to blame the forces of Nature and the uninterrupted advance of the jungle for too large a proportion of the destruction. They do not take due account of the long passage of time. Then those who have made a detailed study of the ruins maintain that vandals were responsible for a considerable amount of damage through their efforts to get at the base of the towers, where it was commonly believed that the priceless sacred relics, jewels, precious metals and stones were buried. They tore out and took away the T-irons which supported the statues or held them

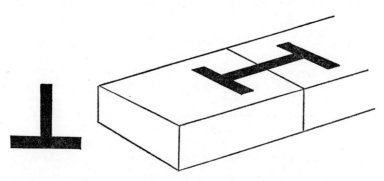

The T-irons which held building stones together

together. Some buildings collapsed through grave defects in the construction, and reference is made to this cause elsewhere. There is no doubt that all these agencies of destruction combined to bring the edifices crashing down.

However, these numerous ruins, broken, shattered, scarred and some half-buried are scattered over a wide area. Yet they possess a wistful, tragic and lasting dignity. What a fabulous city Angkor Thom must have been in its heyday! The network of moats had facilitated the transport of stone and building materials, even if it

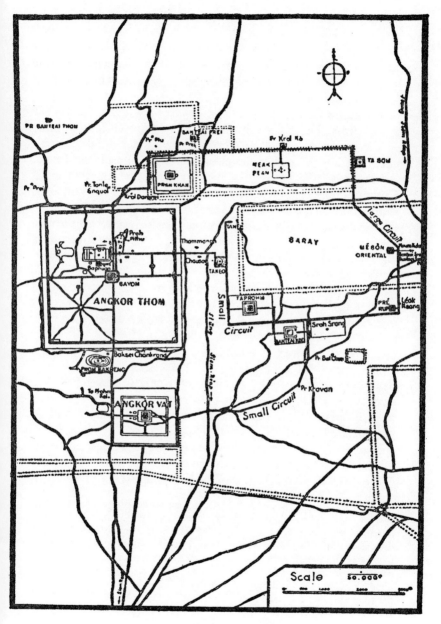

Disposition of the Ruins of Angkor

did not lessen the lot of the slaves for they quarried the rock and sandstone in larger quantities, to load it more quickly. Laterite, limestone, sandstone, hard rock were hewed out in enormous piles until, before Jayavarman's orgy of building had spent itself, the quarries were beginning to dry up, and new sources further afield had to be tapped.

The gateways to the capital rose 60 feet high, the moat was 180 yards across. There were five magnificent gates with the miracle of the Bayon marking the centre of the capital. Inside the vast enclosure are the lovely temples of Banteai Kdei, Neak Pean*, Preah Khan*, Ta Prohm, Ta Nei, Ta Som, the superb Banteai Chmar in the north-west, and many other temples and buildings, some of which are still in an excellent condition.

One crosses a wide causeway which leads over a vast moat to the south gate of Angkor Thom. A dark, forbidding and crumbl- ing wall stretches 8 miles, enclosing the capital. The causeway is bordered by two rows of squatting stone giants representing gods and demons. They support the enormous stone *nagas* in the crooks of their arms, elbows resting on bent knees. This is another repre- sentation of the Churning of the Sea of Milk. When the visitor crossed over the causeway and walked into the city, this action symbolized the entry into the Hindu conception of the universe Each *naga* forms a balustrade for the causeway. Similar *naga* balustrades lead to each of the city's five gates. There are fifty-four giants to each balustrade or 108 to each causeway, making a grand total of 540 in all. They are nearly 8 feet high squatting. Standing, they would be at least 12 feet high. Some faces and limbs have dis- appeared or toppled backwards into the moat. The general effect of these brooding stone faces is quite startling, especially at night. The *naga*-head marks the end of the balustrade. It rears right up on

* Writing of these temples and the stone used for building them and others, Geoffrey Gorer says: "the discovery of soft and easily worked basalt in a quarry a few miles from Angkor, provided the medium through which fantastic dreams could become solid. Every tower became human, looking with four faces over the world; every wall alive with processions, with elephants, with *garudas*, watch towers and flowers like lotuses (Preah Khan) more, stone houses would arise from artificial lakes (Neak Pean); there should be no more death; the stone itself would come alive. There was no limit to the audacity of their conception. Sometimes clumsily, sometimes triumphantly, the buildings took on the forms of gods and beasts, cut out of blocks of basalt piled on top of one another without mortar, overlaying a foundation of laterite." (*Bali and Angkor*)

high. The multi-heads have been exquisitely chiselled, and the flared hoods with the graceful sweep the sculptors have given them are most imposing.

After the comparative safety from snakes at Angkor Wat, it is wise to be prepared when walking among the ruins of Angkor Thom, for many visitors have accidentally disturbed these loathsome creatures with unpleasant results. They like the cool and deserted chambers and libraries and shady ruins. It is an unwise tourist who turns over a piece of stone or masonry, for the chances are that there will be one of them lurking underneath.

The entrance gate is most imposing and quite unusual. The sculptured wings of the gateways beyond the *naga* balustrades represent triple-headed elephants. Their long trunks reach to the ground and are lost among clumps of sculptured lotuses. The elephants decorate the huge, strong flanks of the gate. The towers above are adorned with four huge Buddha faces. Tall, reinforced and massive wooden or bronze doors once protected the city from attack. A huge moat swarming with crocodiles, and behind it the stone wall, and further back an inner wall with a terrace and ramparts for soldiers provided the defence works.

In the enclosure there are a large number of flat buildings. Huge and very heavy rectangular stones lean dangerously, balancing on cracked columns, but some stone lions in a very good state of preservation are still mounting guard on ruined staircases.

Apparently the enclosure was formerly occupied by the royal palaces, court and military administration and priest-cult, as well as residences for the high officials of all services, nobles and courtiers. The main population lived in the suburbs and on the banks of the Siem Reap river as far as the shore of the Great Lake, and close to the two artificial lakes, the East and West Barays.

The most lively and spectacular area of the capital was the Grand Plaza. This was a wide, open place, an enormous and imposing square which was lined with stately buildings. The walls of the Royal Terrace are still covered with a mass of superb bas-reliefs, devoted mainly to animals. It is the most picturesque yet brilliant spectacle in sculpture in the plaza. Close to the Royal Terrace, on the north side is another terrace. This is the Leper King's. Descriptions of this king are conflicting. It has been alleged that the statue represents one of the monarchs who was afflicted with leprosy, but the students of Khmer history and architecture argue that there is no such evidence of disease, other-wise the sculptors with their attention to detail would have shown the ravages on the surfaces of the statue. In actual fact, the king is quite unique in that he bears no resemblance to any other statue of a Khmer king or dignitary.

He is life-size, without sexual organs, and is seated on a stone slab with his right knee propped up as a support for the right elbow, while the left hand, palm downwards, rests on the left leg. It is also said that he represents Jayavarman VII, the founder of Angkor Thom, and that this king actually did suffer from leprosy, which affliction made him take such a compassionate attitude to the sufferings of others that it was a major influence in his stupen-dous programme of hospital building and social service.

However, as always in Cambodia, legends are related by those on all sides who find in them an explanation which satisfies where history fails or is silent.

The following legend is perhaps more plausible than so many of the others. The Leper King in life was a Khmer King who fled the capital a jump ahead of two generals, Vayonska and Thonnit who had plotted to murder him. They quarrelled, and the king in his flight through the jungle, met a holy man who told him that he would overcome both rebels, but that in victory he would find only dirt. However, he was not to despair, for in the mire, he would find jewels of priceless value.

The king disguised himself and fought under Vayonska and killed Thonnit, then turned on the other and slew him. He declared his identity to the troops who acclaimed him. He marched at their head back to the capital, entering by the North gate. Here he was given a rapturous welcome for he was very popular. Then disaster struck. A woman ran in front of his horse which took fright and threw him. She flung her arms around the king and kissed him. The happy, boisterous onlookers were transfixed with horror. Then they fled. In a matter of seconds the triumphal avenue was empty. Even the faithful bodyguard had deserted him. For the woman was a known leper. The common subjects could be so afflicted, but not their king! He was at once dethroned and shut up in a prison cell on the site of the present terrace. The ending was reasonably happy, for his faithful wives dug a tunnel to reach him and lived with him until he died. This love and fidelity were the priceless jewels promised by the holy man.

Some credence is attached to this legend because of the existence of a tunnel there today. The Cambodians take the view that as the historians cannot agree on the origin of the Leper King, this legend is as suitable as any other explanation; moreover, it makes a pleasant story.

One descends a steep and narrow staircase between two walls forming the inner and outer façade of the north terrace. The outer wall is covered with fine bas-reliefs showing the Khmer kings walking in procession above a sea of *nagas* and fish. The inner wall is carved with as much detail and care. Both are fine specimens of Khmer carving and are in an excellent state of preservation, although those on the inner wall are better. The expression on the face of the Leper King suggests that he is well content with his lot.

Many visitors and writers are amazed to find that the sculptors carved such exquisite designs on the wall and then placed a second wall behind it, filling in the space between with earth, but the students of Hindu mythology maintain that this is the pattern of Mount Meru, with the world reaching down into the earth as well as above it.

The inner wall was not discovered by the French archaeologists until some sixty years after Henri Mouhot came upon the ruins, and is therefore a comparatively recent find. One of the most fascinating features about Angkor is the fresh light shed from time to time upon the mystery of the ruins. More data is constantly being produced; the discovery of an important inscription recording some noteworthy event in Khmer history or the find in the jungle of some architectural gem. It would appear that Angkor will continue to arouse interest as more secrets are unearthed.

However, even those who are well disposed towards Khmer legends would surely agree that the king and his wives must have possessed a talent and endurance equal to that of the best sculptors of that time. A more likely explanation was that the original terrace was found to be too small, and so the outer one was added; moreover, the tunnel provided a private entrance to the north terrace by which the king and high officials could come and go without ceremony.

In spite of the crumbling and scattered ruins, the boundaries of the Grand Plaza are not difficult to follow, The imagination conjures up scenes of colourful pageantry which were a frequent event. There were ceremonies and contests, naval and military reviews, massed bands and thousands of spectators.* The numerous artificial pools are full during the rainy season, and beautifully clear. They are Nature's mirrors in which are reflected the tops of the majestic buildings. There are so many that one yields to a compulsive urge to wander from one to another and admire the images. In some there are the reflections of the tall, shattered columns of a forgotten temple which appear to be only a short distance away but quite inaccessible. Once they supported lofty and ornate roofs. Broken steps led from the square, bordered on either side by triple-headed elephants, so constructed that their backs appeared to support the weight.

A million people† once lived in this city and walked, drove or were borne through the streets, passed through the ceremonial gates, watched the sculptors at work. And what a variety of subjects they bequeathed to posterity, although the vast majority centred on religion and the worship of the gods! There was

* Prince Norodom Sihanouk became King of Cambodia in 1944 and abdicated in 1955 in favour of his parents to take over the office of Head of State. In January 1970 he left the country for medical treatment in France. His departure coincided with demonstrations against Vietnamese troops in Cambodia. On March 18 the National Assembly removed him from office. He is now in exile, and may well be the last of the Cambodian kings. He traces his ancestry back to the celebrated Suryavarman II, the founder of Angkor Wat. During his reign festivals and pageants were held which depicted life at Angkor in the time of that king. The author witnessed two such festivals.

The procession was led by Brahman priests blowing the sacred conch shells. They were followed by standard bearers and other officials carrying bundles of rattan, symbol of the king's unifying authority. Drums, actor slaves, attendants in costumes of contrasting colours and carrying gold bowls of scented flower petals, delegations representing the provinces and outlying districts and dressed in period costume, dancing girls, clowns in grotesque masks, warriors with lancers, swords and ox-hide shields, musicians with cymbals and pipes; tumblers and acrobats, detachments of infantry, cavalry with saddle blankets reaching almost to the ground. Ministers rode in palanquins with silver shafts, borne on the shoulders of bearers. There were royal elephants caparisoned in red head covers, their tusks encircled by gold bands, and howdahs in which the king, queen and escorts were seated. High dignitaries with coloured parasols and huge flame-shaped emblems on long sticks formed the royal escort.

At the ceremony of rice planting, the prince wore a long pink and gold cloth tunic and violet sarong, the high spiked and sacred helmet on his head. He reminded his audience of the great victories won by the Khmers in the days of the god-kings and exhorted them to keep alive the memories of the glorious past.

† Some historians put the figure as high as 2 million.

Vishnuloka the King, seated on a throne with his generals below him, or surrounded by the ladies of his court; and the representation of the Sea of Milk with the devils and *asuras* or demi-gods using the serpent Vasuki as a rope which they twined around the base of the allegorical Mount Mandara. And half way down the two lines a god-like figure with four arms. This is Vishnu who changed himself into a huge tortoise to support the mountain. More gods with their female retinues. Another fight between the devils and *asuras* for the possession of the elixir which Vishnu had to drink to ensure mortality. These variations in the myths and legends are refreshing.

However, it is maintained that this was the legend which inspired the Victory Gate, where the stone giants confront the stone gods, with the great *nagas* in their laps. This gate was used by ambassadors and those who had business with the court.

The famous Elephant's Terrace still stands, a long wall, over a half mile in length, in which a magnificent procession of about 400 yards of these huge creatures is seen passing by or hunting in a forest. The central section of this terrace in front of the east gate of the royal palace is in line with the Victory Gate and Phimeanakas. It is ornamented with huge *garudas* with raised wings. Little is left of the palace beyond the gates, carved terraces and flights of steps. The *garudas* take the form of caryatids which were believed to support a royal pavilion which stood in the centre of the terrace and cover a distance of 200 yards. At Angkor Wat, the bas-reliefs depicting heaven are held aloft by *garudas* to give the impression that the palaces are floating in the heavens like the mythical celestial palaces of the gods. The terrace which leads to Preah Khan at Konpong Thom is ornamented with *hamsas* or geese in flight. This is meant to depict the flying chariot of the god of riches which has been stolen by the demon Ravana and which is always depicted on the wings of *hamsas*.

While this magnificent capital of Angkor Thom was being built—Jayavarman VII was determined it would be more illustrious than any previous capital of the Khmer Empire—he speeded up work on a temporary headquarters which he called Preah Khan or 'Fortunate City of Victory' to commemorate his victory over the Chams. At the same time work went ahead on two temples quite close to each other. These were Ta Prohm and Banteai Kdei. The general style of all three is in many ways

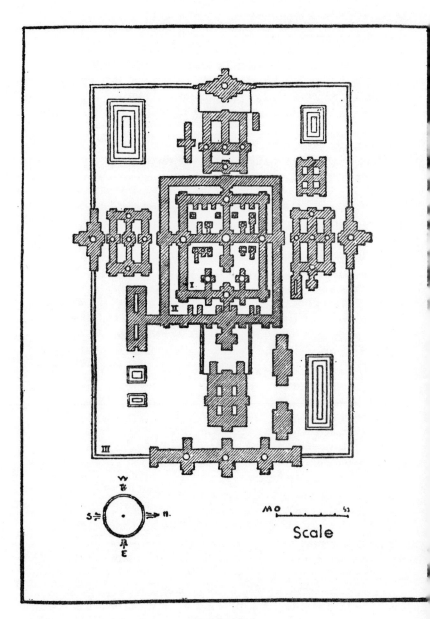

Scale

Preah Khan

similar to that of Angkor Wat, but of course they are smaller. Preah Khan was to be the funerary temple of his father, King Dharanindravarman II. Ta Prohm is dedicated to his mother, and she is represented in the sanctuary in the guise of the spiritual mother of Buddha, which is one of the many examples of Jayavarman's belief that he was the living Buddha.

Preah Khan has been left much in the same condition in which it was discovered by the French, except that walls and ceilings have been strengthened. The central image was enclosed in a temple dedicated to the gods. An inscription on a stele states that there were 430 images, but in the temple precincts there were about 20,000 images in gold, silver, bronze and stone. The upkeep of this temple must have imposed a crushing burden upon scores of thousands for over two centuries. One inscription records that 306,372 servants from 13,500 villages worked there and consumed 38,000 tons of rice annually. A list of twenty-three religious foundations is also inscribed. These were known as *Jaya Buddhamahanatha*, and they were consecrated in many cities throughout the Khmer empire. These included Petchburi, Ratburi and Lopburi, all of which are in Thailand today. Another stele states that "121 rest houses with fire were constructed along the roads which spread out from Angkor to the capital of Champa, seventeen on the road from Angkor to Pimai in the plain of Korat" (in modern Thailand).

There are the familiar towers, moats, libraries and galleries in Preah Khan, but the whole edifice has been damaged so much by the devastating forces of jungle growth that there is little left of its former glory, although it is not difficult to make out the design. Yet is is a strangely beautiful sight with its shrouds of roots, prowling boughs and branches, as well as the galleries from which the trees have taken root and are growing vigorously. A huge, well proportioned flame-of-the-forest tree casts a crimson glow over the ruins.

A short walk leads over a dry moat, then to the crumbling masonry of what was once a stout wall, into a park and on to a temple in the distance. Beyond the ruins of another wall, there is a second enclosure and a smaller park which gives access to the temple. The inner door is framed by two massive columns. The temple is built in three concentric squares, with the sanctuary in the middle. In some ways, the design and construction differs from

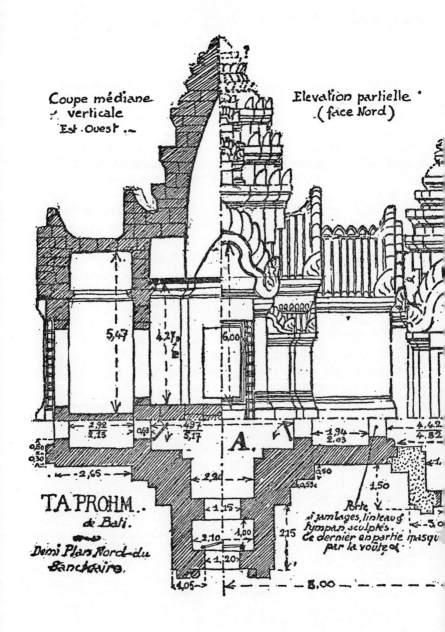

Coupe médiane
verticale
Est.Ouest.–

Elevation partielle
(face Nord)

5,47

4,2?

6,00

2,92 / 3,13

0,63

4,97 / 5,17

1,94 / 2,03

4,42 / 4,82

A.

0,80
0,30

-2,65-

2,20

0,50

2,05?

1,50

1,15

4,00

2,15

TA PROHM..
de Bati.

Demi Plan Nord du
Sanctuaire.

2,10

1,20

20

4,05

8,00

Porte
à jambages, linteau &
tympan sculptés.
Ce dernier en partie masqué
par la voûte

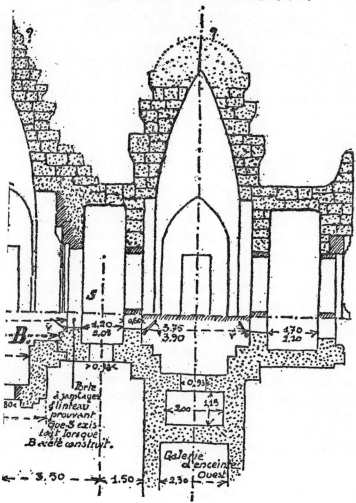

The Temple of Ta Prohm

that of Angkor Wat. That edifice has one enclosing wall. Preah Khan has two. The galleries of Angkor Wat are raised in graded heights, whereas those of Preah Khan are on one level. The reason for these differences is that the king, Jayavarman VII, was a devout Buddhist and was not influenced by Hindu mythology, which required that the central complex of buildings must conform to a pyramid temple reaching to a group of five sanctuaries representing the quintuplet peaks of Mount Meru. There is a cross of chambers, each arm forming one room.

The craftsmen appear to have carved their lines more deeply than has been the case in so many temples. The dancers smile seductively from broken columns or from the prone positions into which they have fallen on their bed of stone. The columns, which were formed in double rows have a forlorn appearance amid the surrounding desolation, yet there are sculptured treasures of outstanding beauty, massive in size and weight which have crashed to the jungle floor. There is so much evidence of vandalism that it is possible that it was inflicted during the anti-Buddhist wave which followed on the death of Jayavarman.

Some of the chambers were entirely roofed over with branches and foliage, and it was only after the most careful examination that it could be seen that in some cases the ceilings had actually crashed, perhaps because of the upward growth and pressure of the trees or because of the tightening pressure of the branches of others.

The exquisitely beautiful temple of Ta Prohm is one of the outstanding marvels of all the Khmer ruins. It has been left in the same conditions as it was when Henri Mouhot discovered it, although, as in the case of Preah Khan ceilings and walls have been strengthened to prevent further deterioration. However, the trees and jungle growth which throughout the centuries have encircled it, distorting the masonry, lifting parts up from the main structure and tilting them forwards at fantastic angles, still remain.

It is very popular with visitors, many of whom comment wistfully that it is a pity that more ruins had not been left in the same state. It is really an amazing spectacle. The roots and branches of several trees, mostly wild fig trees, and the multi-rooted banyan have run riot. They have taken root on tops of towers, in crevices of buildings, and one has the impression that the earth must have called out to them for they have prowled along in search of it—enormous roots which have traversed great distances from the

(*above*) The pediment from above a gateway at Banteai Srei. (*right*) Banteai Srei

(*left*) Khmer sculpture of the
seventh century. (*above*) A
bronze *naga* of the twelfth
century

trunk, reaching across and around huge blocks of rock and stone to probe deeply into the luxuriant earth which has been the elixir of life to them, for they have taken root deeply and grown with increased vigour. The elements made the stone base fertile with the torrential rain which lashed down and penetrated the almost solid green ceiling of the jungle to reach the decaying vegetation and soil. There are trees which have taken root two terraces from the ground. The bombax or silk cotton tree towers up amid the ruins to greet the sky.

It must have been a magnificent temple nearly 800 years ago. An inscription on a stele describes Jayavarman VII as a staunch Buddhist and goes on to say: "the high path which leads to Supreme Enlightenment, the unique doctrine without obstacle to attain an understanding of reality, the law which the immortal honour in the three worlds, the sword which destroys the jungle of the passions".

Another inscription gives us some idea of the size of the army of workers who once went about their employment in the temple, and the amount of room accommodation required. The inscription lists ". . . . eighteen principal officiants, 2,740 officiants, 2,232 assistants, 615 woman dancers, total, 12,640, which comprise those who have the right to lodgings. 66,625 men and women who perform the service of the gods. Total, 79,365." The temple property included a set of golden dishes weighing 500 kilogrammes, a silver service almost as heavy, 35 diamonds, 40,620 pearls, 4,540 precious stones, a great golden bowl, 876 veils from China, 512 silk beds, 523 parasols and 2,387 sets of clothing to dress the statues.

Now pillars, terraces, gables and towers are mixed with trunks or branches or roots of trees, and it is not always clear which of them is giving the necessary support, for they are locked in a twisting, ever tightening embrace. The roots hang like a giant fringe over the façade. The faces of the stone images look as if they have been distorted with pain because of the pressure from the roots. The faces of the Buddha have met the same fate, and in some cases the encircling boughs have made their smile more vacuous.

It is a unique experience to contemplate the results of a duel which has lasted nearly six centuries between the massive stone architectural masterpiece and the forces of Nature. It still retains an irresistible charm, in places an ethereal beauty. There is little doubt that the victory of the jungle would have been complete in the end but for the intervention of Man.

Banteai Kdei, which is close to Ta Prohm, was a rectangular self-contained walled city. It had been built in a park. The city had been surrounded by a wide moat. Paths still lead to the temple. Here, another moat once surrounded it, except at the approaches on the east and west where it is broken by raised causeways leading to the sanctuary. There are many small chambers and scores of little courtyards with doorways beautifully decorated with fine carvings. Spiral scrolls on the panels form a series of designs which are varied and most attractive.

Ta Som is another lovely temple which the French archaeologists have left much in the same condition. Here, bad workmanship must absolve Nature for much of the blame for its decay. The foundations were weak, the huge blocks of rock were assembled with haste and insufficient care, with the result that the temple shifted in parts from the base. Walls have moved from the upright, and the prowling roots and branches found their work of destruction much easier. "A seed dropped by a bird. It grew to a shoot and then to a mighty tree!" So wrote a famous naturalist. A gateway surmounted by a tower, the four sides of which are made up by enormous faces of the Buddha. They stare at the visitor from all sides and give the impression that he is being spied upon by the Enlightened One. But on closer examination, the faces are not those of the Buddha, but of Jayavarman VII, who, already at this early stage in his long reign, believed that he was the living Buddha and proceeded to proclaim his immortal identity as at Ta Som.

One of the loveliest little shrines of all Khmer buildings is Neak Pean. The name means 'curved *nagas*'. It is a temple of exquisite design built on a square island which is dry except during the rainy season. A causeway leads to it from one of the sides. A small oratory, erected on the back of two intertwined *nagas* from a network of basins represents the magic spring which is alleged to cure all ills.

The smaller basins are situated at the four cardinal points. Their original purpose was ritual ablutions. During the reign of Jayavarman VII, the ladies of the court enjoyed an almost entire monopoly of this shrine and gave gold offerings for the privilege. Steps lead down to these basins and along these steps are very small structures shaped like chapels.

The oratory rises from the central basin which also contains statues symbolizing the compassion of the Bodhissatva Avalokitesvara. It has been carved to resemble a lotus blossom.

These lotus blossom towers enjoyed great popularity and the greatest care was taken with design and execution. Those at Angkor Wat are masterpieces of architecture, the one at Neak Pean is beautiful in its isolation. Although archaeologists find errors of planning and defects in craftsmanship in Khmer architecture in general, the lotus towers appear to have received nothing but praise. In Khmer days they possessed a spiritual force, a mystique. George Groslier* wrote: "*Le lotus en est le seul motif identifiable, fleur sacrée par excellence et emblématique des cultes buddique et brahmanique.*"

The oratory at Neak Pean has no interior and its doors are false. Here, the French reconstruction teams are to be congratulated on an admirable piece of conservation for they were obliged to remove an enormous banyan tree from the oratory, and this was accomplished without damage to the structure.

Jayavarman built the beautiful pleasure pool of Sra Sang. It is actually a very large reservoir. There is a stone landing-stage with steps guarded by lions, and a *naga* balustrade running to the water's edge.

Sra Sang was obviously the playground of the rich and influential. Here the courtiers spent much of their leisure time, indulged in water sports and competitions, and intrigued and plotted.

The stone platform must have been used for spectators who came to watch the various events. Pavilions were no doubt erected on it and along the banks.

The landing stage was used for boat races and for processions of royal barges which made their way in stately processions across the lake. Or else, the tiny craft so popular in those days raced across the waters to the cheers of the enthusiastic supporters.

At night, Sra Sang must have presented a beautiful sight with the huge torches lighting up the craft and the pleasure seekers. For the place was a scene of revelry. Here the privileged wended their way from the grey temples. Here, in the comfortable barges of the nobles or in the seclusion of the pavilions, couples paired off and made love, taking advantage of the privacy, which the lake, with its many amenities provided.

* *Recherches sur les Cambodgiens* by George Groslier.

It is not difficult to imagine the jealousy and bitterness which the pleasures of the comparative few at Sra Sang aroused. It was not so much the masses who were seething with anger, but those who were on the fringe.

They were the lesser aristocracy, those of good family but in impecunious circumstances, the artists and scholars whose work and ideas had offended the influential set, either because of their refusal to conform to generally accepted techniques and design, or because they were too independent to observe the frills of court etiquette with its hierarchies, protocol and ceremonial. There were also those who could not or would not buy themselves into the social circle. And so, as in the case of the exclusive temple rites and orgies, there were a large number of discontented but powerful individuals.

Their jealousy and frustration brought them together. They found themselves on common ground, linked by a common bond, although they were ill-assorted bed-fellows There were the young intellectuals and would-be reformers, the wealthy but socially unacceptable merchants, the artists and the young officers, the old and lecherous who flattered the younger element and so stoked the fires of envy. They watched the barges passing up and down Sra Sang, illuminated by gaily decorated lanterns with candles inside, listened to the sounds of revelry, the music and dancing, and they plotted. Some of them were actuated by high motives. They wanted an end to the mad extravagance, but the majority were guided by less worthy intentions. They were excluded from the circle and that was enough.

Suryavarman II also built the temple of Banteai Samre. It stands amid remote isolation, with the lush, fertile jungle advancing on all sides. Yet it is surprisingly well preserved, and furnishes another example where the jungle has not been entirely destructive, but has, in some parts acted as a protective screen. Or else it was constructed with more care and so survived where others collapsed and crumbled.

It has long stone-vaulted galleries surrounding a quadrangle which has a solid wall on one side and open arches on the other sides.

It stands beside the East Baray, and this must have lessened the work of the temple servants. This vast lake and reservoir was built by Yasovarman, who also built 800 artificial ponds, Banteai

Samre must have presented an attractive sight with its reflection cast on the mirror-like surface of the baray.

Archaeologists are of the opinion that the high tower of the central sanctuary of Banteai Samre was a precursor of the later Angkor Wat, and that the architects developed this feature as well as the galleries with the surrounding quadrangles, with one solid wall and open arcades when they designed and built their great masterpiece.

Another temple, Beng Mealear, also built by Suryavarman II, now lies in ruins, and there is little left to show what it looked like. Presumably it was constructed on the same lines as Banteai Samre.

Banteai Chmar is one of the great provincial citadels built by the same king. There was once a huge reservoir outside the main building, similar to the enormous reservoirs at Angkor Wat. The principal buildings were approached by causeways leading to gateways, and bordered by *naga* balustrades. There are still several sanctuaries sculptured with bas-reliefs, including those of naval engagements, but the temple is a mass of fallen columns and broken walls, and the ground is strewn with lichen-covered rock. Little restoration work has been carried out, possibly because the building had deteriorated to such an extent that reconstitution was impossible. This is clearly a glaring example of a great building collapsing through weak foundations and slip-shod workmanship. The place is very desolate, but colonies of monkeys provide a lively welcome. The visitor will find himself peered at from the branches of trees, he will be the subject of lively discussion; large numbers may combine to give an acrobatic and agility display, sometimes culminating in the gift of a coconut thrown with painful accuracy. Banteai Chmar appears to have been taken over by these tireless, gay and mischievous creatures.

The most spectacular edifice erected by Jayavarman is the unique, amazing but grim and forbidding Bayon. It is an architectural wonder and extravaganza in statues and bas-reliefs. When the last stone was laid, the orgy of building initiated by the vainglorious king, now a nonagenarian, came to an end. It was also the last great monument of the Khmers and could be considered a fitting conclusion. An exhausted and bankrupt nation squeezed the last drops from the sponge in an all-out drive to maintain the marvels it had created. It was a superhuman effort and for a few years it succeeded, but as the enormous granaries began to empty,

and the defects in the irrigation system upon which the existence
of the population depended worsened, with a resultant drastic decline in crop yield, its failure was imminent. There were far too
many temples, the number was far in excess of the religious needs
of the people and the cost of feeding a huge army of non-produc-
tive temple officiants was beyond the nation's resources.

Although Jayavarman had devoted his energies to this vast building programme, he had also given his kingdom an excellent network of roads especially constructed on a raised level to combat
the floods. He had built hospitals, rest houses and canals. The latter
were constructed with much greater care than most of his temples.
One in particular, dug from the old capital and 40 miles long to
join with a river proved to have absolutely no error of divergence
from a straight line in that length.

Before concluding this chapter with a description of this Khmer
masterpiece, let us look at those buildings which still survive in
this vast area of devastation. It should be remembered that in
building his new capital, and hauling great quantities of rock from
the Dangrek mountains, he used the foundation of many of the
old ones upon which to construct his new edifices. In some cases
this was an advantage, for previous kings had built with more
care and precision and there had not been the same frenzy of
speed.

In King Indravarman's reign, two delightful temples were built.
These were Prah Ko in 879, and Bakong two years later. A third,
Lolei, was the inspiration of the succeeding monarch Yasovarman,
who reigned from 889 to 900, and to whom we also owe the
temple of Prasat Kravan.

Prah Ko, Bakong and Lolei are three very attractive temples
situated near each other. Prah Ko has six towers which have been
constructed in close rows on a low platform. Bakong is a pyramid
temple where Mount Meru was represented by recessed terraces
built in tiers. The central shrine stands on the summit of the
terraces surrounded by the other towers. The Bakong was a great
advance on all previous temples in design and construction. It
ushered in the beginning of classical Khmer architecture. The
Khmers adopted this style for most of their buildings which
followed, improving and embellishing it. It was a pyramid of
rising steps or tiers, crowned by towers and axial staircases which
led to galleries, entrance pavilions and towers. The ledge is

decorated with a continuous frieze of bas-reliefs—only one panel has survived but it is a work of art. It represents a scene from one of the classical myths. A giant has cut down with one blow an enemy standard represented by a bronze figure carried at the end of a pole. The faces are contorted with rage and hate. It is a fearsome picture and the effect is quite startling. The Bakong was the most imposing of the three temples. It was also the most sacred, for it housed the royal *linga* of King Indravarman. Visitors to Angkor are puzzled by the constant reference to the term 'royal *linga*' especially as the object is sometimes so stylised as to deepen the mystery. Briefly the spirit of royalty was believed to dwell in the *linga* symbolizing the power of the god Siva, set in a pyramid at the centre of the royal city which in turn was situated at the axis of the world. This *linga*, an image, was believed to have been obtained from Siva with the assistance of a high Brahman priest who presented it to the original founder of the dynasty on a sacred mountain. If there was no natural height, an artificial hill would suffice. Jayavarman II was said to have received from the summit of a mountain the miraculous *linga* in which the royal power of the Khmer kings would dwell. When he moved to Phnom Kulen he arranged for a Brahman to instruct his own personal priest in the cult of the god-king.

Jayavarman VII departed from the style of a pyramid temple for this symbol could not be reconciled with his Buddhist faith.

Lolei is a group of four platform towers and, like Bakong and Prah Ko, is built mainly of brick. Stone was employed for doorways and niches. There is some excellent and exquisite carving on the columns and lintels, and among the many charming features of Prah Ko and Lolei are canopied niches flanking ornate doors, some of which are false, each one sheltering a guardian spirit. At the Bakong and Lolei one always finds a large number of Buddhist monks in the vicinity of the temples—their presence is accounted for by a temple in the precincts. Here again, the passage of centuries was bridged, and the saffron robes make a vivid splash of colour among the monuments of the past.

Another temple, Bakheng has an interesting story. It housed the royal *linga* of Yasovarman I when that king moved his capital from Hariharalaya in Roluos to Angkor. New temples were built and many of these are more isolated than others. Bakheng is close to the south gate of Angkor Thom. It is a pyramid temple crowning a hill. The steps are guarded by squatting stone lions on perrons. This new capital was larger than Angkor Thom, and in order to build and maintain it, Yasovarman altered the course of the Siem Reap river. Bakheng was his tomb at his death as it had housed his *linga* in his life. The four long flights of steps were revealed when the French archaeologists were excavating from under the steep slopes of the hill.

Prasat Kravan has five brick towers arranged side by side. The bas-reliefs stand out in sharp relief. The sandstone surface lent itself to more ambitious work and the sculptors produced more intricate designs. Here, Vishnu and his consort Lakshmi stare out from the inner walls of the central shrines.

TEN

The Bayon, Banteai Srei and the Buddha

Two enormous temples, built during the reign of king Rajendra-varman, are of special interest, for they appear to be the last Khmer temples to be built of brick. From this period onwards they were built of stone. These are the East Mebon, built 952, and Pre Rup, 961. They are massive pyramid temples each with five towers grouped on the top terrace. The five towers which form the sanctuary stand on imposing laterite bases. The towers of Pre Rup rise from an imposing laterite platform about 40 feet high and 160 feet wide. The long halls were once roofed with wood and are the forerunners of the later concentric galleries. They extend along the first two galleries. Apart from their huge proportions, their appearance is not attractive. They have taken their full share of the buffeting of Nature and the jungle and the ruins present a forlorn and neglected appearance.

Both have some interesting inscriptions engraved on the steles. Two, at Pre Rup, state: "Her slender, graceful and radiant body, fragrant with the most rare and costly perfumes of the East, clothed in beautiful apparel, triumphs over all the beauty of the god with the arrows speeding—the God of Love."*

The other is dedicated to the king, and says: "To the King who steadfastly bore the earth's burdens, to whom did the King of the Serpents, as if glad to be relieved of his burdens, present the brilliant jewels on its thousand heads, binding them all together with ornaments of gold."

At East Mebon, there is a glowing tribute to the trinity, and Siva in particular. "To Siva, to the Lord of the eternal thoughts, to the One Being who, to satisfy himself by creating, preserving and destroying, divided himself into three supreme gods—he who was born of the lotus, Brahma; he who has the eyes of the lotus,

* Adapted from the French translations of the Sanskrit. For sources, see bibliography.

Vishnu; he who has three eyes, Siva. Three supreme gods on whom the Powers repose." It concludes: "to the blessed Siva let homage be paid. May he bring you prosperity!"*

Yet another declares: "Like the blessing of Spring on the garden, like the day of the full moon, so has she risen, ravishing and splendid in the beauty of her fresh youth. Where could one find another example of her perfect beauty? The base surface of her mirror is not worthy of the face which it reflects. . . . Constantly and without tiring she penetrated into the hearts of men, as if seeking to strike the pirate Love, who lies in ambush within them."*

If these inscriptions are an example of the general theme, then it would appear that King Rajendravarman did not object to the singing of the praises of others. However, he was a broadminded and kindly monarch in comparison with most Khmer kings.

To reach the lovely Banteai Srei, this gem of Khmer architecture, one drives for 20 miles from Angkor over a rough and dusty road, where it is at times very difficult to control the car, swerving and braking suddenly to avoid small boys leading water buffaloes whose massive horn-spans threaten to crash through the windscreen and windows. The latter are kept closed because of the swirling dust. These merry urchins—and some of them cannot be more than 7 years old—handle these huge beasts with competence and ease. A shrill cry, a handful of pebbles flung with unerring accuracy, and the creature comes into line. Barefoot and naked to the waist, they grin cheerily at the oncoming driver, confident of his ability to take such evasive action as will miss them and their charges.

Banteai Srei is one of the finest and most outstanding masterpieces of Khmer architecture. Its remoteness from the capital as well as its isolation no doubt saved it from destruction by the Chams and Siamese. It was not discovered until 1914, when the French archaeologist, Henri Marchal, came upon it. This is not altogether surprising when one looks at the almost solid wall of jungle which concealed it for for so long. It is a thrilling experience to fly over it by helicopter, as well as a beautiful spectacle as the pilot gives a close-up view by skimming the towers.

Henri Marchal painstakingly and skilfully reconstructed this exquisite temple which is really a majestic sanctuary set in an oasis

* Adapted from the French translations of the Sanskrit. For sources see bibliography.

which is surrounded entirely by palm trees, coconuts and banana fronds with the usual jungle trees soaring upwards only a few yards away. Magnificent sculptures line the approaches to the temple. On the causeways which lead to the gates, and on the walls, the guardian statues give the building an added dignity. Banteai Srei is an assembly of sanctuaries, libraries surrounded by the moat.

All the buildings are small, and, what is so unusual, are built of pink sandstone, in some places a delightful reddish tone, This adds immensely to its attraction, for the colour blends exquisitely with the surroundings. The doors to the sanctuaries are quite small and narrow, and the libraries, too, have been constructed on the same reduced scale. The miniature courtyards and staircases are an architectural masterpiece and the proportions are perfect. Such is the immediate impression Banteai Srei makes upon the visitor, and close inspection increases his admiration.

Banteai Srei has an atmosphere entirely of its own. The peace is so profound that one absorbs it, forgets the Khmers and their wars of conquest, the massive monuments they built, their victory gates. It is the pearl of Khmer architecture, and many experts claim that it is not only the most beautiful of all the Khmer temples built in this reign but that it contains some of the finest mural decorations in Khmer art. The temple is unique, and there is nothing in Khmer architecture which can be compared with this charming, miniature building.

The gateway is a portico supported on four plain stone columns. The roof commands immediate notice because of the striking effect provided by the stone beams. The decorations have been sculptured so cleverly along the grain that they give the impression that it is not, in fact, stone, but wood.

Inside the gallery, there is a walled enclosure which surrounds a number of miniature stone buildings in this lovely pink sandstone which provides such a welcome relief from the sombre, dark grey which is a feature of most Khmer temples. The buildings and chapels are in such an excellent state of preservation that it is easy to imagine that they have remained undisturbed throughout the centuries. Unfortunately, this has not been the case. There has been theft on a large scale, and some of the sculptures have actually been taken out of the country to adorn private museums. The reconstruction teams of the École Française d'Extrême-Orient have

made good much of the damage, and have reconstituted the
carving where possible.

Three shrines have been built on a corniced platform and follow
faithfully the contours of the chapels. At the head of a flight of
steps two monkeys have been sculptured in such a posture and
erected in such a position that they appear to fill the role of sentries.
If it were not for their ape-like features, they could well be figures
of men. They sit erect on one knee, the left hand on the lower
thigh. One pair represents the monkey general, Hanuman. He
wears a loin cloth and what is presumably a general's hat. The
expression on their faces is fierce and forbidding, but the variations
and peculiarities in the items of clothing and head-dress provide an
element of light relief. Some wear short pleated skirts and masks of
birds and beasts, and look positively comical, for apart from the
face the body is human. Again, they are in an excellent state of
preservation. The jungle has not destroyed, it has thrown its protective screen around many of the temple buildings.

Two miniature temple libraries of pink sandstone blend with
the shrines. They are delicately carved, with such intricate and
elaborate patterns that one is lost in admiration at the skill, care
and patience of the sculptors. Here there was no possibility of error,
no covering up of any slip with the chisel. The passage of time
would have betrayed it. They worked in a narrow and confined
space, and it could be assumed that this handicap was a challenge
to them to prove that the smaller the medium and the greater the
difficulties the richer their art.

The buildings have all been built close to each other, and this
proximity serves to increase the beauty of the temple complex.
The pediments on the libraries are carved, and it is not difficult to
make out the figures of Hanuman and Ganesh, the elephant god.
Nagas are well in evidence.

In the north library, the iconography is devoted to Vishnu, the
south is the domain of Siva. Sometimes the entire pediment is
given up to one of the gods. These libraries are so small that their
real purpose has been the cause of lively controversy for years.
Sacheverell Sitwell* suggests that "it is likely they were sacred
storehouses like those at Ieyasu's Shrine at Nikko, in Japan". This
is an explanation which many would accept. The exteriors are
richly carved with hooded pediments over the door. These con-

* *The Red Chapels of Banteai Srei*, by Sir Sacheverell Sitwell.

tain a large number of diminutive figures. The motif is the giant Ravana shaking Mount Kailasa. One very beautiful pediment is crowded with figures and woodland scenes. A triple fronton has been carved so ingeniously that it can be mistaken for sandalwood instead of its actual stone. In the top and largest tympanum, the *naga* appears and extends down to the bottom corner where it opens out into the familiar flared, multi-headed cobra head. On either side are more cobra heads which act as ornaments to the roof.

The pediments of the *gopuras*, the lintels and the principal sanctuaries are taken up with scenes from the legends or legendary lives of the two gods. Here there is wide variety of subjects and representation of the mood of the gods.

For example, in one of the tympana above the doors, they sat aloof in majestic isolation or danced or fought, with sentries represented by *devatas* and *dvarapalas*, but inside the sanctuaries the gods are secluded, protected by sentries with heads of animals. Variety is the keynote of the dress and head-dress. Vishnu is sometimes depicted with a diadem on the forehead, decorated with a flower, or the cylindrical chignon; the *devatas* are made to appear more graceful with a chignon surrounded by flowers. Striking exceptions at Banteai Srei are the *dvarapalas*, who elsewhere are decorated with an abundance of precious stones—they are quite unadorned here.

Similarly, the gods on the bas-reliefs and sanctuaries are sculptured without ornaments. It is possible that the court ordered that when the sculptures were complete, real jewels and necklaces should be placed around the figures. However, both *devatas* and *dvarapalas* have been made to look younger and more radiant, and one has the impression that they would look less dignified loaded with jewels and ropes of pearls.

The small chapels present a mystery. It is difficult to decide, with any certainty, their function, although during the centuries which followed on the fall of Angkor to the discovery of Banteai Srei, it appears that they were used by hermits. Today they are in ruins.

One interesting feature of this miniature temple complex is the conflict which has raged between archaeologists as to the date of its construction. Banteai Srei is not the only Khmer temple to be the subject of controversy which in some cases has been protracted and even bitter, but in no case has the period been changed about so much as is the case with Banteai Srei.

One explanation which accounts for much but not all of this controversy is that some archaeologists fixed the date rather too prematurely and were a little embarrassed when later, evidence came to light which disputed it; inscriptions were misread or there were errors in translation. Then the late discovery prompted the experts into making a judgement which was, in the light of later events, a little hasty. This is, perhaps, excusable. The Angkor ruins were discovered in 1861, and it is likely that the French reconstruction teams had, with reason, concluded that by the end of the century they had unearthed all that the jungle had concealed for so long. Henri Marchal's marvellous find in 1914 electrified the archaeological world and its members delved into records and research.

Henri Parmentier* says that it was commenced about the year 967. Benjamin Rowland puts it as late as 1304. Some writers have placed the date of construction at sometime in the last quarter of the twelfth century. Bernard Groslier† gives the year as 967, which was during the reign of King Rajendravarman (944-968) when Angkor became the capital. His father, George Groslier devoted a lifetime to the study of the Angkor ruins, the style of architecture, and amassed a vast amount of records and statistics. This is the date now generally accepted today as the year when these beautiful temple buildings—a toyland, as some writers have described them—were built.

Banteai Srei means 'Citadel of the Women'. There is an air of femininity about the entire edifice. It is charming, exquisite and dainty. In contrast to the huge Khmer temples, with massive towers dominating the landscape, everything here is small. But it is not a reproduction of the more massive buildings. The sanctuary towers are no higher than 20 feet from the ground, but the area of the temple complex is large.

At the time of its construction the Khmers were living in a brief era of peace. The court was leading a life of ease and culture. The capital was a centre of learning. Scholars and artists from all over the region were attracted to it. There were no conquests to com-

---

* *Le Temple d'Içvarapura* (*Banteai Srei*) by L. Finot, H. Parmentier and H. Marchal.
　† *Angkor Art and Civilization* by Bernard Groslier.

memorate. And so Banteai Srei reflected the spirit of the age.

The celebrated Phimeanakas was commenced by King Jayavarman V and completed by his successor, King Suryavarman, This temple is the Golden Tower described by Chou Ta-kuan, where, according to legend, the royal *naga* changed herself into a beautiful woman at night. The king was required to indulge in the pleasures of sexual intercourse with her before visiting any of his wives or concubines. If either party failed to keep the assignation the king would die or disaster would overtake the kingdom.

Most Cambodians do not take this legend seriously as they do some of the others. Those with some knowledge of the ruins point out that the Phimeanakas could not have been a royal palace for such buildings were built of wood, although richly ornamented and decorated. Only the temples were built of stone. What is certain is that the king did go with his retinue to the Phimeanakas, but for the purpose of worship.

It was made up of three laterite storeys, the highest of which was completely enclosed by galleries vaulted with sandstone. Jayavarman VII had the temple restored and incorporated into his new capital of Angkor Thom. His second wife, Indradevi, who was the sister of his first, had an inscription extolling his virtues included in his biography carved on a stele.

It must have been a very beautiful building in the days of Suryavarman, with its lofty terraces and sculptured galleries. It was built in the middle of cultivated parkland. Close to the temple the king built the royal enclosure with the official residence in front, the administrative and domestic quarters behind, and pavilioned gardens surrounded by a laterite wall enclosed by a wide moat.

His wives, concubines and children once lived here, and an inscription records that the earlier king, Yasovarman, taught dances to princesses. There were schools for dancing and music. I came upon several stone temple dancers in the grounds. Some of them smiled up at me from clumps of tropical flowers which gave them a seductive setting.

Life as it revolved around the Phimeanakas was colourful, animated and varied. The wives and concubines found plenty of distractions, for in front of the royal enclosure, the renowned Suryavarman laid out the first Khmer grand plaza. It was a most imposing square, and, although later kings were to add their own buildings such as the Terrace of the Leper King, Suryavarman conceived the plaza. It was a place of beauty and splendour where public festivals were held, and ambassadors were borne through broad tree-lined avenues for an audience with the god-king.

The gateways and walls are now in ruins. Scattered stones lie half hidden in what was once the royal enclosure, but they give some idea of the immensity of the place, and the bold lay-out of the temple buildings. Lakes and pools are close by, with steps leading down to the water.

It was Suryavarman I, the conqueror of Siam who built the Takeo. This is a pyramid temple formed of three terraces and is almost entirely covered with trees and foliage. One of the smaller towers housed the statue of Siva with his wife on his knee.

King Udayadityavarman built a larger temple than those constructed by previous kings. This was the Baphuon, described in an inscription made at the time as a "gold temple on a gold mountain". Nothing like it in size, grandeur or majesty had ever been built before. Among all buildings inside the city walls it is second in size only to the Bayon.

It is unfortunate that it has not been possible to reconstruct the ruins, for the temple would have been one of the outstanding monuments in stone. Its disintegration was not due so much to the encroaching jungle combined with the destructive force of the torrential rains, or to the thieves, vandals, rampaging Siamese or Vietnamese, but rather to the fearful blunders of the builders and the undue haste of an ambitious and impatient king. He ordered that a high, artificial hill be erected, not only in accordance with tradition, but from his own sense of grandeur and vanity. It had to tower above the capital and the work had to be completed without delay.

Insufficient time was allowed for the earth to settle and find its foundations. The massive, heavy blocks of stone were hoisted into position and the building went up with excessive haste. For a few years all went well. King Udayadityavarman had his beautiful, funerary temple, the Khmer capital and a new showpiece for the illustrious visitors and erudite scholars who travelled from all over South-east Asia and the Far East, and in particular from Peking, to study its design and architecture. Then ominous cracks began to appear. The building could not be shored up. Its terrific weight hastened its end. The pride of the Khmers collapsed. And its disintegration was so complete that the French archaeologists who had accomplished wonders in the reconstruction and reconstitution of other ruined masterpieces found that they could do little. Today it is a scene of utter devastation and desolation.

An uneven path leads between two depressions and ruined pyramids of terraces. There is still enough left of the temple for one to visualize a once stately entrance with antechambers leading off. There are the remains of an encircling wall. The entrance leads to a low viaduct which continues to the second enclosure, where there is a long rectangular pond.

The towers have long since crumbled, and the terraces are overgrown with jungle growth and trees whose roots have made merry sport with the weak structure, twisting and levering the stones off one another, and away from the upright. Bas-reliefs are still in evidence, and there are superbly carved scenes from the *Ramayana* and *Mahabharata*.

All such religious buildings had to be a fitting place for the abode of the particular god. The sculptures were usually touched up with gilt and bright colours. The ceilings and doors were of carved wood, often of intricate design, and gilded. They combined artistic skill with strength, but their main purpose was to hide the bare stone and embrasures.

The god image was usually framed in gold, and a collection of articles for use in connection with the ritual of worship were placed at its feet. The soaring towers flaunted a god trident. The god images were stylized, and the design was unchanged. It was widely believed that as they represented one or other of the trinity they were perfect, and any attempted improvement was an offence against the god. There was little danger of damage, for they were housed in magnificent sanctuaries and brought out only on rare occasions to be shown to the public. No Khmer statue in stone depicted movement, but more freedom was allowed in bronze. It appears that there were as many images in this medium as in stone, in which case there must have been wholesale looting over a long period. Fortunately a few were found and are in the National Museum in Phnom Penh. They are of exquisite loveliness and design.

Large numbers have been found all over the former Khmer empire and are now in private museums. There, unfortunately,

12

they are likely to remain. Reports which have been sent back to Phnom Penh tell of the high degree of craftsmanship.

The bronze founders cast very large idols as well as small, fragile statues. As in stone, the design was usually religious. There were images of the trinity and the Buddha. Khmer bronze reached its peak in the second half of the ninth century, when it is claimed that it had attained a standard of perfection unsurpassed in Asia. At that time, the casts were either very small or very large. They continued to be produced right up to the fall of Angkor. The process adopted was *cire-perdue*, or 'lost wax'. The bronzes* were cast from wax moulds which were then broken up. The *patina* or incrustation that covers the bronzes is not always green. Some are black or very dark brown, and the difference is accounted for by the alloy used.

The usual procedure was to use a mixture of new metal with pieces of composition. In addition to brass, an alloy known as samrit, which was a conglomerate of gold, copper and silver was employed. Tin, zinc, lead and bismuth were also used.

An enormous reclining Vishnu was found in the East Mebon temple, and the Vishnu in the Musée Guimet, Paris, is one of the largest Khmer bronzes.

From the eleventh century there was a drastic change in the style of the bronze work and a deterioration in the quality of the craftsmanship. From the fourteenth century until the fall of Angkor the general standard was poor. This falling off was due to several causes.

Large bronzes became less fashionable. The vogue was for a statue under 12 inches in height. The people wished to have them in their houses as evidence of their piety, for the great majority depicted the gods. With the massive programme of temple building the sculptors in stone were fully occupied and quickly became rich; the bronze workers found that there were fewer opportunities for their work and so the master craftsmen took on fewer apprentices. There was, however, an increased demand for bronzes among the people coinciding with the Buddhist wave which swept the country under Jayavarman VII.

Religious fervour was it its height. The now comparatively few

---

* The bronze medallions of Pissano were cast by *cire-perdue*, and it is claimed that their very high standard was due to the use of wax moulds. All early bronzes were cast from wax models and moulds.

bronze workers were besieged with orders and many had neither the training nor the skill to undertake the work. Large numbers were turned out, again all small, but they were mostly ugly and the craftsmanship was very bad. Those of good quality were few.

Although the objects were small, they had to be decorated. With such a reduced size, this was difficult, but love of the ornate overruled any objections the artists may have made. The result was that they were lacking in dignity and were even grotesque. However, the bronze workers were enjoying a boom, and few took pains over their work. To be fair to them, the time factor was against them. In any case, the fact that the idol represented this or that god or demi god was what mattered most to the purchaser, and so they were installed in their private sanctuaries.

The artists concentrated on single objects which they depicted in pose and movement. The costumes were similar to those worn in the stone statues.

Some gods have been cast in bronze but are of indeterminate origin as they have no duplicate in stone. In some figures bronze proved to be a more suitable medium than sandstone because their weight did not disturb the balance.

Two great temples were, until the empire fell, the pride of the Khmers. One was Angkor Wat, the funerary temple of Suryavarman II or Vishnu incarnate; the other, the Bayon, funerary temple of Jayavarman VII, Buddha incarnate. Angkor Wat was later to become a Buddhist shrine like the Bayon.

Angkor Wat has survived in much of its former glory. It represents a miracle of reconstruction, and the view from the causeway is very little different from that which greeted Chou Ta-kuan in 1296. The Khmers are justifiably proud of it. It is the *raison d'être* of the Cambodian tourist industry. All over the country one comes across the ubiquitous imprint of the temple—on the national flag, on other flags and decorations, on official note paper. Huge photos and colour prints adorn the walls of airline offices and tourist agencies; smaller reproductions illustrate travel brochures.

There is barely a paragraph about the Bayon. Unhonoured, unsung, not a flag, not a photo.

A striking contrast is provided by the descriptions of Pierre

Loti,* written in 1912, and Chou Ta-kuan† over 600 years earlier.

The former tells us: "I stared up at the tree-covered towers which dwarfed me, when suddenly my blood curdled, for I saw an enormous face looking down on me, and then another face over on another wall, then three, then five, then ten, appearing from every direction, and all had the same faint smile."

Elsewhere, he describes his visit to Angkor Thom and his path which led to the Bayon. "One had to hack out a path to reach this monument. The jungle entwined it in a giant embrace, strangling and crumbling it. Enormous fig trees had taken root all over it, growing and spreading up from the tops of the towers, making pedestals of them. Some of the doorways were completely matted with a thousand hairy roots."

Today, when coming upon the Bayon, with its dark, grim, for-bidding—even frightening—appearance, the description of the Chinese visitor gives a feeling of immeasurable relief which raises the spirits and gladdens the heart. For it is possible to visualize it in the days of its majestic, colourful splendour, especially when climbing crumbling stairways, scrambling from plinth to plinth and leaping from terrace to terrace.

From the days of Jayavarman VII, its founder, until the capital was abandoned two centuries later, it was the showpiece of Angkor architecture, the glory of the Khmers and the reason for the existence of Angkor Thom as the capital. The approach to it was startling in its magnificence and ceremonial, but it was always awe-inspiring, and frightening to many.

The moat was teeming with crocodiles, and this must have made the bravest feel a little uneasy, even if they had to walk with fitting dignity across the spacious, ornamented causeway. This was bordered by *naga* balustrades, which the Chinese visitor des-cribed as "holding in their arms as a parapet a serpent with nine heads, and looking as if they were trying to prevent its escape".

At the end of the causeway was the entrance to the city and to the great temple. Here the triple-headed stone elephants projected out of the massive wall. Here, the golden‡ bridge, eight golden Buddhas, here the Bayon, where the giant Buddhas gazed across

* *Un Pèlerin d'Angkor*, by Pierre Loti.
† See Chapter 5.
‡ Presumably gilt, which was used in large quantities for ornamental pur-poses.

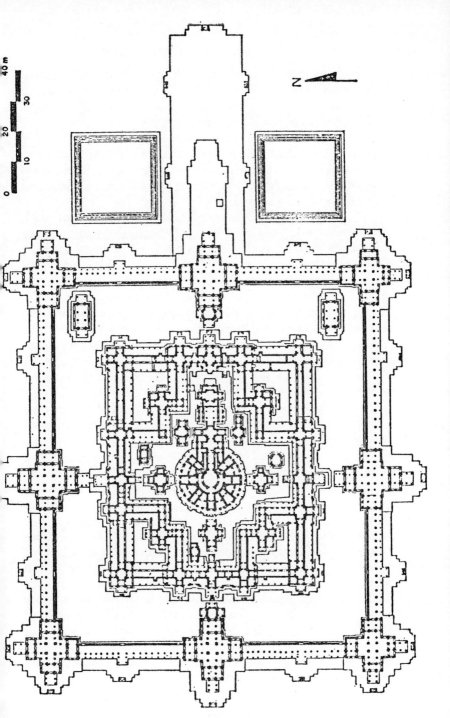

The Bayon, Angkor Thom

the city in all directions. Wherever the people looked, wherever they walked, a Buddha watched them. They stared at it when the day began until it ended. It was the image of the Buddha, of their god-king, and the reason for their existence.

Today one climbs a broad, stone stairway. Stone lions, which no doubt were placed there in the past to represent guardians, have toppled from their pedestals and lie in odd positions, some completely undamaged. The visitor passes between them and through the main entrance.

This was the great funereal temple of Jayavarman VII, built with the toil, sweat and blood of scores of thousands of slaves. They hauled the heavy, cumbersome rocks from quarries 20 miles away. They tugged and heaved, rigged up jigs and hoists to move them into the required position, driven on by their cruel, exacting and relentless masters—who, themselves were expendable if work did not progress at the speed which satisfied their superiors. The stones were conveyed over raised or built-up roads so that there would be no enforced delay because of the floods. The lot of some slaves—those whose sandstone quarries were closer to the site of the temple—was less hard. However, these wretches died in their thousands, mostly through jungle fevers, exhaustion and stones which fell and crushed them. Their bodies were flung on carts which took them a short distance to where they were unloaded and left to the vultures and wild beasts.

The Bayon was the Temple of Death, but it was also to be a monument of human endeavour and great achievement in the arts. It is said that it took a generation to build, and it was obviously constructed to last, for today it stands almost defiant in its completeness and stark solidity after 800 years.

One of the most impressive features of the Bayon is the bas-reliefs which are on the lowest terrace. There is almost a mile of them, and they cover the entire wall surface. They are rich in variety, and many have been produced with a delicacy of touch and accuracy of detail which are a tribute to the talent of the sculptor, although others have been executed with a less polished finish. The mind reels in astonishment at this superb pageantry of plaques, and at the number of sculptors who were employed on this vast work. There is a marked difference in the subject matter of those on the outer wall and those in the inner gallery. The former is taken up mainly with historical events and everyday life, while the inside has been devoted to the world of gods and myths.

As the Khmers left no written records, these bas-reliefs are a legacy to their descendants. Here, they have bequeathed the story of their lives and also the fantasies and legends.

They show the life of luxury of the privileged classes. In barques and barges, lovely maidens laze away their leisure hours. The boats are fashioned in the shape of a *naga* with the hood reared and flaired. There are boats with canopies of embroidered awnings and cushions. Bronze chariots are decorated with carvings and jewels, royal howdahs are richly caparisoned. Dancing girls are shown making themselves more beautiful. Nobles are attacking wild beasts with poisoned darts, playing polo on small ponies and hunting. The king's superhuman powers are represented in such scenes where he has thrown an elephant to the ground and is holding it by one of its hind legs. The same fate has been meted out to a lion in spite of the jostling of his courtiers. He is also seen in council with his ministers, or receiving the homage of his officials. There are scenes from the wars, with soldiers fighting in ships or from elephants—doubtless an epic skirmish of the Royal Regiment of Elephants.

The religious side is brought out with due solemnity. Long processions of priests, with the influential Brahmans distinguishable by their beards and robes, bands playing, and troupes of *apsaras* or dancing girls on their way to the temple.

The Chinese element is well in evidence. Their racial features, as distinct from those of the Khmers, are well portrayed. Here they are all traders, and in one bas-relief they are seen arriving by boat with their merchandise.

The pictures of everyday life are fascinating. There are women cooking with wide pans over open fires, combing their hair; a child being deloused; a pregnant woman about to give birth, with the midwife in attendance; two men playing what appears to be chess; two more roasting a pig; farmers bringing their produce to market in panniers suspended from a pole slung across their shoulders; market women selling their wares to bargaining customers. There is cock-fighting, dancing, fishermen hauling in the catch, a woman selling food at an open-air stall, peasants planting rice paddy, a cow suckling its calf. Light relief is provided by the large number of *apsaras* who contrive to look so lovely, enticing and seductive.

Animals are plentiful; they are shown moving happily and playfully through a number of bas-reliefs; but, as if to remind the spectators of the ever constant danger, a realistic picture shows a youth being set upon by a tiger, and a crocodile biting a swimmer in two.

It all happened in Angkor ten centuries or more ago, although the Bayon was constructed later, between A.D. 1181 and 1218. But life has not changed much with the passage of time (characteristically with a rural population that lives off the land). Khmers were shipped thousands of miles from their native land to fight in French legions during two world wars, and from reports they appear to have acquitted themselves well. One wonders what memories they brought back with them of the ghastly strategy of human slaughter in an alien country where the cold and mud contrasted with their sunshine and blue skies. Yet on their return, they adapted themselves without difficulty to a resumption of their peasant life. The water buffalo plodded through the paddy fields, the peasant lowered his huge nets into the klong which flowed past his wooden house, young men re-entered the monastery for short or long periods. Little was changed except that the liberation and independence movements were about to bring about a resurgence of national pride.

There is much that is confusing about the Bayon. French experts who have studied the edifice maintain that too much was crowded into an area which, although spacious, could not accommodate all the structures without overcrowding.

The lower gallery is a maze of porches and terraces; the courtyard has two libraries. The visitor passes down dark and gloomy corridors of different levels, with narrow chambers. This was possibly a dreaded walk for those summoned centuries ago to appear before the priests or officials of the court.

The next terrace housed the sacred chamber. The Khmer architects must have been pleased with their work for they had enclosed it with squares each one larger than the one immediately higher. The central shrine which is situated under the highest tower is shut in and very dark. Access is not easy and can be perilous for there are narrow and deep gorges in close proximity. This is just one of the errors of construction. Another reveals that the terraces are not large enough for the towers. The base of the main pyramid is too low, for it almost touches the colonnades of the terrace below, with the result that there are very narrow passages instead of spacious galleries. What galleries there are were so hurriedly constructed that they are small and dark.

Rumours persist today of priceless treasures being sealed in a walled-in crypt deep under the central sanctuary, and that the most drastic measures had been taken on the orders of Jayavarman VII to ensure that the secret of the hiding place was not revealed. Even the high priest had his tongue torn out, and all the slaves who had built the crypt were garrotted and buried in deep ditches under the outer walls so that they would not only be silenced for ever, but that their spirits would guard the approaches to the temple as long as the stone faces on the towers kept their vigil. However, the sacking of the capital by the Siamese was so complete; they were in occupation of the city for several months, during which time they had ample opportunity to extract by torture any information they needed as to the site of buried treasures. This makes it difficult to attach any importance to the stories one hears today. Moreover, after the Siamese had left, marauding bands descended on the devastated city smashing and wrenching apart to take anything of value.

It is possible that some of the wealthy classes buried their own private fortunes when the fall of the capital was imminent, and that they hoped to dig them up when the Siamese departed, but thousands were killed and a large number transported to Siam, with the result that the owners never came back to claim them. Any potential gold digger who tried to penetrate the thick jungle growth would quickly become pessimistic about his chances of finding any caches.

The view from the top terrace is quite breath-taking. It is both stupendous and fantastic, for even the dramatic, colourful language of the guide books does not prepare one for such a spectacle. Some 200 stone faces look out from fifty-four stone towers rising 150 feet from the ground. The towers are each carved with gigantic faces on all four sides, representing the omnipotence of Jayavarman VII who surveyed his capital and his empire. He built the temple to house the Buddha and ended up by believing himself to be the reincarnation of the Enlightened One. Hence the statues were his images!

The heads are crowned with jewelled diadems. Long earrings hang from their ears—which are very large, for the faces are 8 feet

high. Pearl necklaces encircle their necks. Two hundred faces of
Jayavarman VII, the greatest of all Khmer kings, a megalomaniac,
a god-king who believed that his subjects accepted him as such.

Such was the Bayon, situated right in the centre of Angkor
Thom. It was in itself a miniature kingdom, just as the capital city
of Angkor Thom constituted a small replica of the universe. From
this great edifice, four avenues led off in four directions ending
in four magnificent gates which set off its splendour and its imposing height. It was here in 1933 that an enormous statue of the
Buddha was found, probably hidden by the faithful monks when
there was a swing back to the trinity—in this case Siva more than
the others.

As a unique religious monument, it is a magnificent and awe-
inspiring spectacle, but the atmosphere is depressing. It is dark and
gloomy, and it is difficult to rid the mind of the thoughts of the
cruelty and suffering which had continued for so long in this vast
building where in so many places the sun did not enter.

The Bayon has been the subject of lively controversy among
architects and archaeologists since its discovery, but the majority
take the view that it is the most magnificent of all Khmer monuments within the walls of Angkor Thom, the capital. Angkor Wat
is, as previously stated, outside the walls.

Geoffrey Gorer* said of it that "one of the greatest miracles of
the Bayon is that it stayed erect at all, much less surviving as it has
done, the joints of the stones are placed directly above one another
so that the weight above caused the structure to gape and give."

It still gapes and gives, but it still stands. The huge edifice has
fifty-four towers rising to a height of 150 feet. The two vast
reservoirs which were built on either side of the avenue leading to
the Eastern gate must have given the temple a magnificent setting
in the days of the empire. Apart from their utilitarian value and
necessity, the surface reflected the glory of the temple and its
surroundings.

Its design and construction has confused the experts. They
expected it to conform to the principles of a Buddist sanctuary in
accordance with those of its founder who was the most devout
Buddhist who ever ascended the throne of the Khmers.

However, the Bayon does not entirely follow the accepted
pattern. Angkor Wat has a moat in accordance with the traditions

* *Bali and Angkor* by Geoffrey Gorer.

of the Hindu trinity. Angkor Thom, of course, had a moat which was crossed by a causeway, but the Bayon has no moat or surrounding walls. Then, when the plan is studied carefully, it would appear that the original design was that of a pyramid temple, like earlier religious buildings dedicated to the trinity and raised in three receding storeys.

It is possible that having made this concession to long established custom, Jayavarman VII decided that he had gone far enough and decided to go all out and make it a predominantly Buddhist sanctuary. What had already been constructed would either be lost or absorbed into one vast building dedicated to the Buddha and his own deification. He may have been feeling his way at first, then confident that no one would oppose him, had thrown his support behind Buddhism. And so, in place of the five central sanctuaries which were a feature of the other temples, notably Angkor Wat, he built the staggering total of fifty-four. The stately terraces became mere corridors between these huge, crowded towers. He had super-imposed Buddhism upon his funerary temple. And the existence of characteristics of the trinity side by side with the Buddha caused the mystery.

Parmentier* says that the monument gives a weird impression of hoarding and overcrowding. The towers rise right next to each other, the buildings are too close for easy access and the courts are mere pits without air or light. He points out that between the second gallery and the central complex, there is only enough space for dark passages which are repellent, sinister. This, he argues, is a grave architectural blunder.

The space between the foundation of the central mass and the pediments over the doors of the lower gallery would hardly allow a sculptor's chisel nor the wielding of a hammer so that the decoration stones of the terrace have had to remain unfinished, whereas the decorations on the opposite side are complete. Moreover, the top paving of the terrace in some places forms a ceiling over the passageways below, and the position of these stones has had the effect of destroying the excellent sculptures below.

There is always an uneasy feeling of being watched, even followed. It is inexplicable, but it exists, and it is a sensation which

* Le Temple d'Içvarapura (Banteai Srei), by L. Finot, A. Parmentier and H. Marchal.

many visitors share. Of all the Khmer temples, the Bayon to this day has an element of the supernatural about it. For some reason it is more silent than the other large temples, even when there are visitors passing up and down. Perhaps the mass of the over-crowded buildings absorbs the noise. The complex is so massive, yet one is so often shut in, confined in a narrow, dark space.

Wandering over its vast conglomeration of gloomy corridors, through the deserted galleries and libraries, there is an irresistible impulse to glance furtively behind; and although no one is visible, one senses another presence. The feeling may be foolish—and in any case once outside, it quickly passes—but the company of friends is welcome when visiting the Bayon.

ELEVEN

Evolution and Reconstruction

With the death of Jayavarman VII carving in stone virtually came to an end. The pageant of building passed, and a tired nation sat back to contemplate the wonders which adorned its capital while visitors from afar came to admire the panorama of edifices. No more temples of any importance were built by the Khmers. No temple was built by any of the succeeding kings to house the royal *linga* despite the move away from Buddhism led by his successor, Iayavarman VIII. It received little support during his reign and those who followed him were quick to realize that such action was unpopular. The support of the masses for Buddhism was now overwhelming.

The death of Jayavarman VII marked the end of an era. Henceforth the sculptor's chisel and hammer were employed mainly on building a few stupas for the nobility, and in carving inscriptions. They appear to have attracted little notice at the time. Khmer architecture underwent a spectacular transformation. Buddhism required the public worship of the Buddha, and so large wooden pavilions were erected, and these took the place of the massive temples in which the Khmers had prayed for centuries. Throughout that long period the god had been housed in a narrow sanctuary. Now it was on view in the huge wooden pavilion, and surrounded by figures and ornaments.

The successful Siamese invasion of A.D. 1431 rang down the curtain on this last stage of religious building. And during the life of the empire it had included almost every form of monument As Francis Garnier wrote: *"La civilisation Khmère entre le VIIIe siècle et le XIVe siècle, période pendant laquelle le Cambodge se couvre d'une multitude de monuments de toutes sortes, temples, monastères, villes, palais, ponts, etc., montre une puissance royale solidement établie, une organisation politique très développée et surtout une richesse et un luxe poussés jusqu'à l'excès."* A firmly established royal power, a well-developed political organization, wealth and luxury carried to excess!

Both these great forces were dying.

Finally the Khmer kings and the population turned their backs on the glories of the past. In his book *Le Cambodge*★ E. Aymonier gives an eloquent account of "*l'état de plus en plus misérable de ce malheureux pays*".

The sculpture they left behind is staggering in its diveristy and mood. Almost every conceivable subject was represented on the walls of their temples. They include palace life, army, the river and sea craft used, the unfolding of Khmer history, animals, jungle life, mythical birds and beasts, trades and crafts, religion with its rites, heaven, hell, male and female clothing and head-dresses, music, dancing, etc.

The imagination boggles at the amount of rock which was used for the building of these edifices. Jean Commaille† says that three kinds of material were generally used— limonite which "*habituel-lement designé en Indo-Chine sous le nom de pierre de Bien-Hoa', le grès* [sandstone] *et le bois. . . .*" Brick had been used in less frequen-ted places. . . . "*Sur certains points peu fréquents au Phnom-Chisor, à Loley et sur le Phnom Bak-Keng, par exemple, nous rencontrous la brique mais son emploi ne s'est pas généralisé.*"

It is most unlikely that he was thinking of the heavy burden borne by the slaves when he gave the locality of the rock. "*La limonite et le grès entrant dans la composition des édifices des deux Angkor et des temples voisins proviennent des montagnes de Koulen, situées à plus de 30 kilometres, dans la direction est nord-est.*" Twenty miles away!

There were eight different styles of Khmer architecture between the ninth century and the beginning of the thirteenth—when, as stated, building ceased.

The Roluos covered the last quarter of the ninth century and produced Preah Ko in 879, Bakong in 881, and Lolei in 893. Bakong was the first sandstone temple mountain, although the tower sanctuaries are brick. The lintels are richly carved foliage designs, and the decorations on the colonettes which are now octagonal are more intricate and finished. The tympanum is taken up with figured scenes which extend underneath light buildings.

★ *Le Cambodge*, by E. Aymonier (Professor of Cambodian at Saigon) 1875.
† *Guide aux Ruines d'Angkor*, by Jean Commaille.

It is in the Roluos style that the sculpture of human figures in architecture of a religious nature begins to develop. The men are bearded and wear skirts with a few pleats in front, girdles and jewelled diadems. The women are dressed in a plain skirt with pleats. There are lions, Nandi the reclining bull and the *naga*. The *naga* is perhaps the most outstanding example of evolution in architecture for here it is in a very crude form to be developed into the magnificent balustrades centuries later at Angkor Wat.

The Roluos type also produced such innovations as the *gopura* or arched gateway leading to the precincts of the temple, concentric enclosures surrounding the central group of towers, and libraries, the purpose of which is still in doubt but is believed to be for the safe keeping of sacred manuscripts.

The next style was that of Bakheng, which was brief, covering the last years of the ninth and first quarter of the tenth centuries. Here the temple mountain and sandstone towers exist together. The lintels are plainer. Ornamentation has in most cases been executed on sandstone and the result is pleasing. The statues are highly stylized. All sides of the colonettes are decorated with a leaf which is flanked by two half leaves.

Koh Ker followed on Bakkeng. It represents the 'massive' approach to Khmer architecture; very large buildings, huge statues, a style which was much more decorative than those preceding it. The temple mountain occupies a vast space and is surrounded by long halls.

The style of Banteai Srei which produced the East Mebon, Pre Rup and Banteai Srei was distinguished by the variations in size and the diversity of the art and sculpture. The temple mountain has assumed an even greater importance if judged by size alone. There were long timber-vaulted halls, on its lower terraces. The East Mebon and Pre Rup are the last of the plastered brick monuments. The lovely lintels of Bantei Srei are a great improvement both in technique, intricacy of design and diversity on previous styles. The figures decorating the walls are set in graceful recesses. This style, which covered the third quarter of the tenth century, was bold and imaginative, yet elegant.

The style of the Kleangs extended over the remaining years of the tenth and the first quarter of the eleventh centuries, and is famous for the Phimeanakas, Takeo and Preah Viharn temples. The temple mountain was for the first time built entirely of stone

The Sanctua

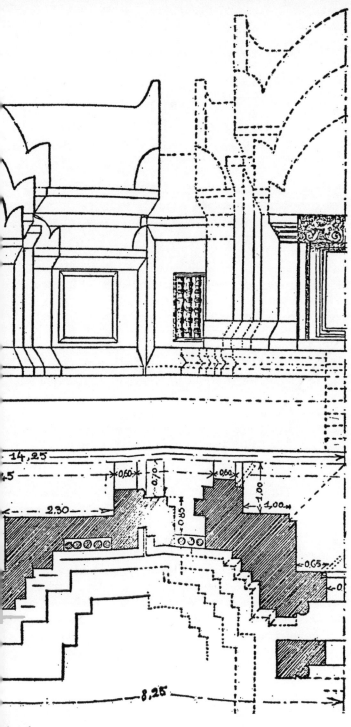

ah Viharn

and has developed still further. It has concentric sandstone, vaulted galleries on the terraces and axial pavilions. The lintels are quite austere, and with the head of a monster in the middle they make a striking contrast to the exquisite working in those at Banteai Srei. The colonettes are decorated with small, serrated leaves and the lines on the dresses of the female figures are more finely drawn.

The next style, that of the Baphuon, occupied the middle of the eleventh century. The outstanding buildings were the Baphuon and the West Mebon. Here the temple mountain was built to massive proportions. Figured scenes decorate the lintels. The tympana are mostly covered with plant motifs. The scrolls are covered with foliage. The sandstone bas-relief is back in favour and small panels are set up over the entrance pavilions. One outstanding characteristic of the Baphuon style is the rich variety of decoration. The bas-reliefs have a prominent place especially in the illustration of episodes of the Ramayana and Mahabharata.

The celebrated Angkor Wat style follows and its period is the first half of the twelfth century. Here the temple mountain reached the most advanced stage of its evolution. It was the culmination of all previous endeavours and experiments to attain perfection. There are concentric galleries on each terrace, vaulted stairways and corridors, and an entire gallery of bas-reliefs. This period occupied the first half of the twelfth century and the architecture and sculpture progressed throughout the half century. For example, the leaves on the leaves were replaced by little circles of small leaves. The temple dancers are more seductive in appearance with their flowered robes and jewels.

The end of Khmer architecture came with the Bayon style, which is identified with the last quarter of the twelfth and first quarter of the thirteenth. Banteai Kdei, Ta Prohm, Preah Khan, Ta Som, Banteai Chmar, Bayon and the royal terraces are the outstanding achievements of this period.

It was characterized by huge temples and the multi-towered Bayon, the Giants' Causeway which, with the *naga* balustrades, symbolized the Churning of the Sea of Milk. The enigmatic Buddhist smile appears on the faces of the temple dancers and other figures. Indeed, the half closed eyes and smile are the distinctive signs of the Bayon style.

Khmer architecture and sculpture has been a subject of lively controversy since the discovery of Angkor just over a century ago.

Possibly the most balanced judgement is that of Bernard Groslier, who has devoted a life-time to the study of the ruins and as an authority is, as it were, to the manner born, for his illustrious father, George Groslier held among other offices those of Directeur des Arts Cambodgiens and Conservateur du Musée du Cambodge.

In his *Angkor Art and Civilization*, he says that the corbelled roof continues to be used "although it is nothing more than an im-improvized method of roofing, bearing the heavy weight and restricting the rooms to gloomy passages. There is a glaring lack of originality in the planes, always the same right-angled arrangement of towers and galleries which vary only in number, and better or worse lay-out. . . . In spite of all this, the Khmers achieved perfection along their own lines or proved themselves the greatest architects in the whole of Indianised Asia."

The reconstruction work carried out by the French archaeologists deserves the highest praise. The results are amazing and must have exceeded the wildest hopes of the early workers and pioneers. There was an enormous amount of research and paper work which had to be carried out before the temples could be reconstructed and reconstituted from the masses of stone and heaps of rubble. Fragments of inscription on shattered steles were deciphered and put together to give the history of the king or the story of the temple. In some cases missing pieces were given up as lost and then found in unexpected places, some were buried deep under the earth. Some sections and figures had to be reconstituted. The historians, the Sanskrit scholars and the archaeologists worked in close co-operation and called in a large number of experts in many different fields.

When at last the temples were cleared a new danger arose. The sandstone rapidly began to crumble. Fortunately they quickly realised the cause. Although the jungle had done its full share of destruction, the surrounding trees and foliage which had grown so thickly during the centuries had acted as a screen to the buildings. Now that this protection was removed, deterioration was threatened by the ravages of a more deadly enemy. This was the water-borne bacilli.

Fortunately the scientists were able to meet the new danger. The ruins were dismantled where necessary, and reconstituted on a strong concrete base, surrounded by drainage pipes. The affected parts were treated with antibiotics with excellent results.

Perhaps a word of praise is not out of place for the many prisoners who toiled in the jungle removing and carting away the trees and vegetation. It is certain that they toiled under far more humane conditions than the slaves of the days of the god-kings.

The technique employed in the reconstitution of the temples and buildings was an example of *anastylosis*. This is a Greek word meaning re-erection. The French learned it from the Dutch, who had ruled much of the Indonesian Archipelago from the early part of the seventeenth century and had acquired considerable experience in this work. Briefly it is a method of extracting ruins from a jungle and assembling the stones so that the final result is that of the completed jigsaw pattern.

The Angkor temples as they stand today are a tribute of their long, arduous and patient work and the success which crowned it.

Bibliography

ENGLISH

L. P. Briggs, "The Ancient Khmer Empire", Transactions of the Amer. Philosophical Soc. Vol. 41, Philadelphia, 1951

H. C. Candee, *Angkor the Magnificent*, H. F. and G. Witherby, London, 1925

E. H. C. Dobby, *South-east Asia*, University of London, London, 1951

J. F. Embree and L. O. Dotson, *Bibliography of the Peoples and Cultures of Mainland South-east Asia*, Yale University, New Haven, 1950

M. Giteau, *Khmer Sculpture and the Angkor Civilization*, Thames and Hudson, London, 1966

G. Gorer, *Bali and Angkor*, Michael Joseph, London, 1936

D. G. E. Hall, *A History of South-east Asia*, Macmillan, London, 1968

B. Groslier and J. Arthaud, *Angkor Art and Civilization*, Thames and Hudson, London, 1957

M. Macdonald, *Angkor*, Jonathan Cape, London, 1952

H. G. Quaritch Wales, *Towards Angkor*, Harrap, London, 1937

Sir Osbert Sitwell, *Escape with me*, Macmillan, London, 1963

Sir S. Sitwell, *The Red Chapels of Banteai Srei*, Weidenfeld and Nicolson, London, 1966.

FRENCH

E. Aymonier, *Le Cambodge*, E. Leroux, Paris, 1900–1904

A. Barth, *Inscriptions sanscrites du Cambodge*, Imprimerie Nationale, Paris, 1885

R. Baradat, "*Les Samre ou Pearr, populations primitives de l'ouest de Cambodge*", *Bulletin de l'École Française d'Extrême-Orient*, Hanoi, 1941

A. Bergaigne, *Inscriptions sanscrites du Cambodge*, Imprimerie Nationale, Paris, 1893

J. Brengues, "*Notes sur les populations de la région des montagnes des Cardemones*", Journal of the Siam Society, Bangkok, 1906

J. Boisselier, "*La Statuaire Khmère et son évolution*", Bulletin de l'École Française d'Extrême-Orient, Saigon, 1955

G. Coedès, *Les États hindouisés d'Indochine et d'Indonésie*, Histoire du Monde, E. Cavaignac, Paris, 1948

G. Coedès, "*Inscriptions du Cambodge*" (6 vols.), Bulletin de l'École Française d'Extrême-Orient, Hanoi and Paris, 1937–54

G. Coedès, L. Finot, V. Goloubew, "*Le Temple d'Angkor Wat*" Bulletin de l'École Française d'Extrême-Orient, Paris, 1929–32

G. Coedès, "*Les Capitales de Jayavarman II*", Bulletin de École Française d'Extrême-Orient, Paris, 1928

G. Coedès, *Un grand roi du Cambodge Jayavarman VII*, Phnom Penh, 1935

G. Coedès, "*La tradition généalogique des premiers rois d'Angkor*", Bulletin de l'École Française d'Extrême-Orient, Paris, 1928

G. Coedès, *Pour mieux comprendre Angkor*, A Maisonneuve, Paris, 1946

Doudart de Lagrée et Francis Garnier, *Voyage d'exploration en Indochine effectué pendant les années, 1866, 1867, 1868 par une Commission Française*, Hachette, Paris, 1869

P. Collard, *Cambodge et Cambodgiens*, Éd. Géographiques Maritimes et Coloniales, Paris, 1925

J. Commaille, *Guide aux Ruines d'Angkor*, Hachette, Paris, 1912

L. Delaporte, *Voyage au Cambodge*, Delagrave, Paris, 1880

H. Dufour et G. Carpeaux, *Le Bayon d'Angkor Thom*, E. Leroux, Paris, 1910

L. Finot, H. Parmentier et H. Marchal, *Le Temple d'Içvarapura* (Banteai Srei), Van Oest, Paris, 1926

L. Fournereau et J. Porcher, *Les Ruines d'Angkor*, E. Leroux, Paris, 1890

M. Giteau, *Histoire du Cambodge*, Didier, Paris, 1959

M. Glaize, *Les Monuments du Groupe d'Angkor*, A. Portail, Saigon, 1948

V. Goloubew, "*L'âge de bronze au Tonkin et le nord d'Annam*", Bulletin de l'École Française d'Extrême-Orient, Hanoi, 1941

P. Gourou, *La Terre et l'Homme en Extrême-Orient*, A. Colin, Paris, 1940

B. Groslier, *Angkor et le Cambodge au XVIe siècle après les sources portugaises et espagnoles*, Annales du Musée Guimet, Paris, 1958

G. Groslier, *A l'ombre d'Angkor*, A. Challamel, Paris, 1916

G. Groslier, *Eaux et Lumières*, Éditions Géographiques Maritimes et Coloniales, Paris, 1931

G. Groslier, *Recherches sur les Cambodgiens*, A. Challamel, Paris, 1921

R. Grousset, *Histoire de l'Extrême-Orient*, Annales du Musée Guimet Paris, 1929

S. Lévi, *Indochine*, Éditions Géographiques Maritimes et Coloniales, Paris, 1931

Pierre Loti, *Un Pèlerin d'Angkor*, Calmann-Lévy, Paris, 1912

H. Marchal, *Guide Archéologique aux temples d'Angkor*, Van Oest, Paris et Bruxelles, 1928

F. Martini et S. Bernard, *Contes populaires inédits du Cambodge*, G. P. Maisonneuve, Paris, 1946

G. Maspéro, *Un Empire Colonial Français, l'Indochine*, Van Oest, Paris, 1929–30

G. Maspéro, *Le Royaume de Champa*, Van Oest, Paris, 1928

C. Meyniard, *Le Second Empire en Indo-Chine*, Société d' Éditions Scientifiques, Paris, 1891

A. Migot, *Les Khmers, des origines d'Angkor au Cambodge d'aujourd'hui*, L'avenir du passé. Le Livre Contemporain, Paris, 1960

H. Mouhot, *Voyages dans l'Indo-Chine, Cambodge et Laos*, Hachette, Paris, 1868

J. Moura, *Le Royaume du Cambodge* (2 vols.), E. Leroux, Paris, 1883

H. Parmentier, *"Modifications subies par le Bayon au cours de son exécution"*, Bulletin de l'École Française d'Extrême-Orient, Paris, 1927

A. Pavie, *Voyages dans le Haut-Laos et de l'Indochine. Mission Pavie*, Mission Pavie, Paris, 1900

Paul Pelliot, *"Mémoire sur les coutumes de Cambodge"*, Vol. II, Bulletin de École Française d'Extrême-Orient, Paris, 1902–11

P. Pelliot, *Mémoire sur les coutumes de Cambodge de Tcheou Ta-kouan*, A. Maisonneuve, Paris, 1951

Index

M